TWENTIETH CENTURY
INTERPRETATIONS

Maynard Mack, *Series Editor*
Yale University

NOW AVAILABLE
Collections of Critical Essays
ON

All for Love

The Frogs

The Great Gatsby

Hamlet

Henry V

The Iceman Cometh

Samson Agonistes

The Sound and the Fury

Twelfth Night

Walden

TWENTIETH CENTURY INTERPRETATIONS
OF

Adventures of
HUCKLEBERRY FINN

TWENTIETH CENTURY INTERPRETATIONS
OF

Adventures of
HUCKLEBERRY
FINN

A Collection of Critical Essays

Edited by
CLAUDE M. SIMPSON

Prentice-Hall, Inc.   *Englewood Cliffs, N. J.*

A SPECTRUM BOOK

Contents

PART TWO—*View Points*

Introduction

by Claude M. Simpson

Mark Twain began *Adventures of Huckleberry Finn* sometime in 1876 and finished it in the summer of 1883. The first burst of energy resulted, he said, in some four hundred pages of "Huck Finn's Autobiography," which he reckoned as "very nearly half done." Twain went on: "I like it only tolerably well, as far as I have got, and may possibly pigeonhole or burn the MS when it is done." Evidently his enthusiasm flagged about the end of chapter sixteen, where the steamboat rams Huck and Jim's raft; it appears that Twain didn't see clearly where his story was going, and, as was his usual practice, he put the manuscript aside. His own allusions to the progress of the novel suggest that he worked on it at several periods, sandwiching it in with parts of *A Tramp Abroad, The Prince and the Pauper,* and a number of other projects which he never finished. Bernard DeVoto, in *Mark Twain at Work,* has argued that Twain took up the Huck Finn manuscript again only after his return to the Mississippi River in 1882, a trip designed to furnish fresh material for *Life on the Mississippi.* More recently, however, Walter Blair, making a minute study of the inks and paper which Twain used during the seven-year period of composition, has assembled evidence to suggest that Twain wrote the Grangerford-Shepherdson episode (chapters seventeen and eighteen) in 1879-80. The point is significant—it discounts the earlier theory that the novel lay lifeless until Twain's revisiting old sights "filled up the tank" and enabled him to proceed with the memorable succession of episodes on the lower river. But Twain's trip was contributory if not crucial: it clearly reinforced his memories, and, as can be seen from parallels between *Life on the Mississippi* and *Huckleberry Finn,* it focused his attention sharply on characters, folkways, turns of speech and the physical background, for which tenuous origins may occasionally be found in earlier notebook jottings. The documentary evidence plainly shows that Twain rapidly set down the last half of the novel at his Elmira, New York, summer home in 1883. Blair believes that Twain had already written chapters nineteen through twenty-one (which introduce the king and the duke), but whether before or after the river trip is uncertain.

For some months following this fruitful summer, Twain worked over the manuscript (reconstructing the details definitively is made difficult by incomplete drafts, including typescripts). He polished it, modulated the tone, and rewrote it extensively. The work was meanwhile subjected to the close scrutiny of his friend W. D. Howells, and to what Susie Clemens called "Mama's expergation." A number of passages were softened, sometimes on Twain's own initiative, sometimes at the suggestion of his advisers. A few notable excisions can be regretted. He had lifted the entire Raftsmen chapter out of the *Huckleberry Finn* manuscript for *Life on the Mississippi* and did not restore it, because the novel was already longer than *Tom Sawyer* and he had plans for exploiting the two books as a pair. We can regret also the loss of a part of Colonel Sherburn's speech in which he castigated the would-be lynch mob for the way it would treat unfortunate women "lowering themselves to your level to earn a bite of bitter bread to eat." But even when gentility was imposed on barefaced language, Twain's basic intentions were seldom obscured.

By the late spring of 1884 the novel was ready for the printer. Twain had become accustomed to marketing his books through canvassers, and *Huckleberry Finn* was not to be released, he insisted, until 40,000 subscriptions had been obtained. He could control the details of promotion and sales because he had recently set up his own publishing house, Charles L. Webster and Co., with his nephew nominally in charge. Twain's barrage of instructions would have daunted most men, but young Charley made his way deftly among explosive orders and contradictory suggestions. He succeeded to the extent that his agents in the field sold some 30,000 copies of *Huckleberry Finn* before publication, and he contracted separately for the Canadian and English editions.

Publication was scheduled for late 1884 in all three countries, but in the midst of printing the American edition, one of the illustrations was discovered to have been so defaced that it had become obscene. Repairs took time, especially in the large stock of bound copies, and though the mishap generated inevitable publicity which may have attracted curious buyers, American publication was delayed until mid-February, 1885, some three months after the issuance of the book in England and Canada. It continued to enjoy a steady sale after publication and soon took its place among Twain's most popular books. Only within the past generation, however, has *Huckleberry Finn* been singled out from all Twain's other work and ranked among the few great books produced in America.

Howells' position, briefly excerpted in our pages, is perhaps typical of informed criticism around the turn of the century. Despite his fond-

ness for *Huckleberry Finn,* and despite his shrewdness in linking it to
the frontier tradition long before Brooks or DeVoto, he hesitated to
prefer it above *A Connecticut Yankee in King Arthur's Court,* and he
reserved his greatest affection for *Personal Recollections of Joan of
Arc.* Another point of view still popular links *Tom Sawyer* and *Huckleberry Finn* as a homogeneous pair. In this judgment they are both
boys' books, to be treasured for their harmless mischief and melodramatic excitement, their nostalgic account of an almost timeless
world into which one can escape from most of society's prosaic limitations. Seen in this light, *Huckleberry Finn* is most truly typified by the
opening and closing episodes in which Tom Sawyer directs the make-
believe as he had done in the earlier novel. Huck thus remains a
secondary figure, dominated by the ingenious inventions of Tom's romantic imagination. Unfortunately, such a reading deprives *Huckleberry Finn* of any serious meaning and reduces it to a sentimentalized
view of a boy's world, spiced-up by pseudo-problems. Even today many
"adapted" versions of the novel have been manufactured to eliminate
the controversial passages or to simplify the text for a hopelessly in-
fantile audience.

To most twentieth-century critics, however, the similarities between
Huckleberry Finn and *Tom Sawyer* are less significant than the differences. Twain's decision to make Huck Finn a first-person narrator
crucially shifted the focus. No longer is it a somewhat detached view
of young adolescents as rendered by a distinct authorial voice; it is
instead the direct and generally unmediated vision of Huck himself,
the skeptical and pragmatic outsider. We are asked to see and judge
the antebellum world through Huck's perceptions of it, but, more im-
portantly, that world assumes its reality through Huck's language.
What Twain has done within the limits of an easy colloquialism is to
fuse immaturity and shrewdness, producing a magically plausible consistency of viewpoint. Huck is an unlikely hero, his language an unlikely vehicle for subtlety of nuance and delicacy of perception. Yet
the achievement, primarily imbedded in unconscious irony, is un-
doubtedly one of the chief elements of the book's greatness. Walter
Blair in *Native American Humor* and Kenneth Lynn in *Mark Twain
and Southwestern Humor* have documented Twain's debt to the tech-
niques of pre-Civil War frontier humorists. But Twain transformed
the vernacular narrator from a half-caricatured bumpkin to a decep-
tively complex figure on whom the novelist depends for his total effect.
In so doing, he transcended the received tradition, as James M. Cox
and other essayists in this volume have shown. It is the strong colloquial voice and the controlled point of view which Hemingway doubtless had in mind in *Green Hills of Africa* when he praised *Huckleberry*

Finn as the beginning of modern American literature. And Faulkner in a picturesquely ungrammatical sentence made essentially the same point when he observed that "Twain was all of our grandfather."

Huckleberry Finn lends itself to scrutiny by those critics who search for archetypal patterns, beginning with the fundamental motif of the journey.[1] As the scene moves between river and shore the book offers us an anatomy of life itself. The rich procession of characters illustrates the vagaries of human nature, and Huck's judgments, sympathetic but incisive, become our means of knowing both the world and Huck himself. For other critics the book is an analogue of the initiatory rites through which a boy becomes a man—an attractive thesis seriously limited by the closing chapters which compromise a hitherto "maturing" Huck. For at least one critic the relationship between Huck and Nigger Jim has approached violation of the taboos of latent homosexuality which a Freudian reading makes glaringly clear (when aided by one or two grotesque misreadings of language and milieu). More plausible is a post-Joycean reading which sees the book as a search for a father, sadly recognizing the inability of any of the father-figures to play their role adequately. Still another symbolic pattern emerges in one critic's analysis of Huck's improvised family histories—most of them defensive strategies to disarm suspicion in alien territory—which suggest a touching desire to identify himself with a family group. Fantasy must yield to reality, however, and we note that Huck is obliged to account for his isolation by recitals full of hair-raising calamities that have killed off his kindred.

A central theme frequently explored in modern criticism of the book is the quest for freedom which animates Jim literally and Huck figuratively. Leo Marx has been particularly concerned to show Huck's growth in social awareness, beginning with a moment of commitment when Huck shouts, "They're after us," and makes common cause with Jim. One observes, however, that midway through the novel Twain dropped this theme, which had suggested an underlying unity, and instead, took up the king and the duke who provided him with a more immediate way of exploiting the episodic river adventure. Certain it is that once the raft has gone beyond the mouth of the Ohio, the Pokeville and Bricksville episodes ensue without reference to an

---

[1] Lionel Trilling and T. S. Eliot among others have discussed the river as highway (see Leo Marx's essay below); ritualistic aspects are treated by James M. Cox, "Remarks on the Sad Initiation of Huckleberry Finn," *Sewanee Review,* LXII (Summer, 1954), 389-405; Leslie Fiedler's Freudian reading is contained in his "Come Back to the Raft Ag'in, Huck Honey!," *An End to Innocence* (Boston, 1955), 142-51; the search for a father is touched upon in Kenneth Lynn's "Huck and Jim," *Yale Review,* XLVII (1958), 421-31; Eric Solomon's "*Huckleberry Finn* Once More," *College English,* XXII (December, 1960), 172-78, discusses Huck's improvised family histories.

escape from slavery. In the presence of the confidence men, Huck and Jim largely become passive figures. As spectators or reluctant accomplices they endure rascality at close range, but not without canny insight into the impostors and the public they prey upon.

Because the events in the lower river are picaresque episodes leading to no inevitable conclusion, Twain seems to have faced a structural crisis in ending the novel, especially if he were concerned with a central core of meaning to which everything should contribute. Already in the Wilks episode Twain's extemporizations threatened to become excessive; fortunately he resisted a notebook suggestion that the genuine Wilks survivor be identified by popping out a glass eye on the back of which his name would be engraved. Twain had proposed elephants for the final sequence, and managed to do without them, but some of his devices are almost as desperate. Still, his resolution of plot difficulties actually brought greater unity to the book than might have been anticipated. The "evasion" sequence has, however, become a battleground for critics.

Almost all who have enjoyed the closing episode have pointed to Twain's thoroughgoing satire of dungeon literature typified by *The Man in the Iron Mask*. But despite the serious undercutting of Tom Sawyer's appeals to "the best authorities," the farcical details have continued to need defense. Near the mid-point of the century both Lionel Trilling and T. S. Eliot justified the reintroduction of Tom Sawyer on the ground of symmetry: a balanced effect results from finishing the book on the opening note and allowing Huck to recede into the background. Both critics went on to speak shrewdly of the mythic properties of the river, the moral quality of Huck's responsibility, the masterful style in which the book is cast. But attacks have continued to multiply, reinforcing Hemingway's flat assertion that the final episode was "cheating." Leo Marx's essay, stating the case for and against Trilling and Eliot, contains a strong counterstatement which has been highly influential. Marx holds that the book, having moved from make-believe into a serious world where Huck wrestles agonizingly with important social and moral issues, is betrayed by the return to buffoonery and grotesque farce. For all the anti-romantic satire and the plausibility of Tom's leadership, the integrity of Huck's character is violated, and all of his growth during the novel is ignored as he lapses back into an older role.

One of the results of Marx's critique has been to focus increasing attention upon Nigger Jim, who begins as something of a stock minstrel woolhead and emerges from this stereotyped role fully individualized. Jim not only achieves considerable dignity, as several of our essayists demonstrate, but he is to a large extent the instrument of Huck's growth. He is also, of course, responsible for evoking a world rich in superstition and folk-belief, portents and cures, weather lore and divination. It is within the darkness of this primitive cultural matrix that Jim and Huck develop a fraternal relationship (embarrassing to those critics who find it condescending to put a fourteen-year-old boy and a middle-aged man on equal footing). Their relationship is not perfectly realized, but Huck's single lapse into selfishness results in one of the novel's finest moments when he "humbles" himself.

On occasion the book's mood is idyllic, and nowhere is the language so simple and eloquent as in Huck's description of daybreak on the river at the opening of chapter nineteen. The peace is the vulnerable peace of withdrawal, however, threatened by any intrusion from river or shore, that is, by contact with a social order which, though Southern, more and more stands for a universalized view of mankind. The contrast between detachment and engagement—sometimes oversimplified by the metaphors of river and shore—has been a fruitful source for analysis of the novel's implicit values. Moreover, this odyssey, although it does not lead to freedom but to an indeterminate close, helps us to define the degree to which man may achieve inner emancipation within the confines of human fallibility. Seen in this light, Huck's two debates with his conscience are of the greatest significance, and our essayists have analyzed them more rigorously than other passages in the book.

For both Richard Adams and Gilbert Rubenstein the unity of the novel is indicated by pervasive moral concerns which give purpose and direction to the otherwise picaresque episodes. James Cox, who also considers the book organically consistent, finds us disliking the conclusion because it disturbs the "moral complacency" we may have felt at Huck's decision to steal Jim. Cox, in the essay reprinted here, emphasizes patterns of inversion which go beyond trading a disapproved Southern conscience for an approved Northern one, and he interprets the last ten chapters as Twain's way of rejecting the tyranny of any conscience. Such a position, here subtly argued, is not the only explanation of Twain's strategies, but it is a challenging departure from other arguments attacking or defending the final episode.

The success of *Huckleberry Finn* lies in the fact that it has miraculously managed to transcend most of its limitations. Its language is vernacular, raised to an uncommon power of effectiveness; its milieu is heavy with local color, but wrenched free of condescension; its hero is a poor-white isolato whose simplicity of vision never blinds him to innate truths; its dedication to adventure assures us surface excitement which cannot obscure an underlying critique of human nature. Twain builded better than he knew. He could never again quite duplicate the triumph.

PART ONE

Interpretations

The Artist as American

by Bernard DeVoto

The kernel of *Huckleberry Finn* is in a speech of Huck's toward the end of *Tom Sawyer*. At the foot of the dead-limb tree t'other side of Still-House branch, he doubts the value of finding buried treasure. "Pap would come back to thish yer town some day and get his claws on it if I didn't hurry up, and I tell you he'd clean it out pretty quick." "Old Times on the Mississippi" contains a passage as integral with Huck's journey as anything in his book, and *Life on the Mississippi,* written over the period when Huck was gestated, has many incidents on their way to fruition.[1] The Darnell-Watson feud is the Granger-ford-Shepherdson trouble in chrysalis, a desultory tale told by a passenger as the *Gold Dust* passes through the chute of Island Number 8. On the upstream voyage as yet anonymous strollers forecast David Garrick the younger and Edmund Keen the elder. John A. Murrell's inheritors hint at revenge in the staterooms of a wrecked steamboat and other creatures of midnight presage the turmoil of search and escape through underbrush. Nor are these volumes the only ones in which pupal stages of incidents in *Huckleberry Finn* may be observed: most of the books that precede have passages of premonition. Why not? It was a book he was foreordained to write: it brought harmoniously to a focus everything that had a basic reality in his mind.

The opening is just *Tom Sawyer* and pretty poor *Tom Sawyer* at that. Huck's report of his emotions while ghosts are talking to him in the wind is a promise of what is to come, but Tom Sawyer's gang commenting on *Don Quixote* lacks the fineness of its predecessor. Dis-

"The Artist as American" by Bernard DeVoto. From Mark Twain's America *(Boston: Little, Brown and Company, 1932), pp. 310-320. Copyright 1932 by Bernard DeVoto. Reprinted by permission of Houghton Mifflin Company. The essay has been abridged for this volume.*

1 Critics who enjoy dealing with the unconscious mind as the womb of art are offered such passages for amusement. I reluctantly confess, however, my fear that they will not indicate a father fixation, Mark's incestuous love of his sister, a forgotten reading of Nathaniel Wanley, or zoöphily.

cussions of ransom and Tom's exposition of Aladdin's lamp are feeble; such finish as they have comes from Huck's tolerant but obstinate common sense, here making its first experiments. But no flavor of the real Odyssey appears until Miss Watson forbids him to avert by magic the bad luck made inevitable by spilled salt, thus precipitating his trouble, and he immediately finds in the snow the impression of a boot heel in which nails make a cross to keep off the devil. . . . It is expedient to list here the book's obvious faults. After a first half in which, following the appearance of old man Finn, no touch is unsure, Mark's intuition begins to falter occasionally. When the Duke has Louis XVII learn a Shakespearian speech compounded out of Sol Smith and George Ealer, high and poetic reality lapses into farce. (Predictably. The humorist's necessity to write burlesque had frequently ruined fine things in the earlier books.) The King's conversion is weakened by his use of pirates instead of the neighborhood church which his predecessor Simon Suggs had more persuasively employed. (Predictably. The necessity to carry a joke into cosmic reaches had betrayed him often enough before.) Huck's discourse on the domestic manners of royalty is a blemish. (Extravaganza had diluted satire in many earlier contexts.) Huck's confusion when he tries to lie to the harelipped girl is perfunctory. (Improvisation had substituted for structure sufficiently often in Mark's previous fiction.) The concluding episodes of the attempted fraud on the Wilks family are weak in their technical devices—the manipulation required to postpone the detection of imposture, for instance, is annoying. Thereafter the narrative runs downhill through a steadily growing incredibility. The use of ghosts, the deceptions practiced on Aunt Sally and Uncle Silas, the whole episode built around the delivery of Jim from prison—all these are far below the accomplishment of what has gone before. Mark was once more betrayed. He intended a further chapter in his tireless attack on romanticism, especially Southern romanticism, and nothing in his mind or training enabled him to understand that this extemporized burlesque was a defacement of his purer work. His boundless gusto expended itself equally on the true and the false. . . . Predictably. It has been observed that he was incapable of sustained and disciplined imagination. One could expect it no more reasonably here than in *The Innocents Abroad.*

So, though I regard comparisons as worthless in æsthetics, the obligation of a critic of Mark Twain rests on me to point out these selfsame faults in the only American novel which even enthusiasm can offer to dispute the preëminence of *The Adventures of Huckleberry Finn.* Much more identity than has ever been noticed in print exists in the careers of Mark Twain and Herman Melville, whose minds were as antipathetic as religion and reality or the subjective and the objective worlds can be. Similarly, Jonathan Edwards's successor, when he came to write his masterpiece, plentifully anticipated the errors of Mark Twain and went beyond them. *Moby-Dick* has, as fiction, no structure whatever. Its lines of force mercilessly intercept one another. Its improvisations are commoner and falser than those in Huck Finn. It does not suffer from burlesque (exuberant vitality had no place in Melville's nature) but its verbal humor is sometimes more vicariously humiliating than such passages as Huck's discussion of kings—a miracle, no doubt, withheld Mark Twain from the mere jokes habitual to him. And, though Melville could write great prose, his book frequently escapes into a passionately swooning rhetoric that is unconscious burlesque. He was no surer than Mark, he was in fact less sure, of the true object of his book, and much less sure of the technical instruments necessary to achieve it. That much of weakness the two novels have in common. It is convenient to point out, this much having been said, that they are otherwise antipathies. *Moby-Dick* opposes metaphysics to the objective reality of *Huckleberry Finn*. It is a study in demonology, bound to the world of experience by no more durable threads than a few passages in the lives of mates, harpooners and sailors who are otherwise mostly symbol or mist. They were the book's disregarded possibility of great realism. Melville preferred to sigh through eternity after the infinite. It is a search which has an eternal value for some minds. Other minds, if they look to fiction for values of time instead of eternity and of the finite instead of the infinite, are likely to relinquish the *Pequod's* voyage toward fulfillment of man's destiny and prefer a lumber raft's voyage down inland waters after no more ambitious purpose than to see what the world is like.

The title announces the structure: a picaresque novel concerned with the adventures of Huckleberry Finn. The form is the one most native to Mark Twain and so best adapted to his use. No more than Huck and the river's motion gives continuity to a series of episodes which are in essence only developed anecdotes. They originate in the tradition of newspaper humor, but the once uncomplicated form becomes here the instrument of great fiction. The lineage goes back to a native art; the novel derives from the folk and embodies their mode of thought more purely and more completely than any other ever written. Toward the beginning of this preface it was asserted that the life of the southwestern frontier was umbilical to the mind of Mark Twain. The blood and tissue of *Huckleberry Finn* have been formed in no other way. That life here finds issue more memorably than it has anywhere else, and since the frontier is a phase through which most of the nation has passed, the book comes nearer than any other to identity with the national life. The gigantic amorphousness of our past makes impossible, or merely idle, any attempt to fix in the form of idea the meaning of nationality. But more truly with *Huckleberry Finn* than with any other book, inquiry may satisfy itself: here is America.

The book has the fecundity, the multiplicity, of genius. It is the story of a wandering—so provocative a symbol that it moved Rudyard Kipling to discover another sagacious boy beneath a cannon and conduct him down an endless road, an enterprise that enormously fell short of its model. It is a passage through the structure of the nation. It is an exploration of the human race, whose adjective needs no explicit recording. It is an adventure of pageantry, horror, loveliness, and the tropisms of the mind. It is a faring-forth with inexhaustible delight through the variety of America. It is the restlessness of the young democracy borne southward on the river—the energy, the lawlessness, the groping ardor of the flux perfectly comprehended in a fragment of lumber raft drifting on the June flood. In a worn phrase —it is God's plenty.

The arrival of Huck's father lifts the narrative from the occupations of boyhood to as mature intelligence as fiction has anywhere. The new interest begins on a major chord, for old man Finn is the perfect portrait of the squatter. Behind him are the observations of hundreds of anonymous or forgotten realists who essayed to present the clay-eaters or piney-woods people, as well as a lifelong interest of Mark Twain's. It is amazing how few pages of type he occupies; the effect is as of a prolonged, minute analysis. There is no analysis; a clear light is focused on him and the dispassionate, final knowledge of his creator permits him to reveal himself. We learn of him only that he had heard about Huck's money "away down the river," but a complete biography shines through his speech. This rises to the drunken monologue about a government that can't take a-hold of a prowling, thieving, white-shirted free nigger. The old man subsides to an attack of snakes, is heard rowing his skiff in darkness, and then is just a frowsy corpse, shot in the back, which drifts downstream with the flood.

Something exquisite and delicate went into that creation—as into the casuals of the riverside. Mrs. Judith Loftus is employed to start Huck and Jim upon their voyage. She is just a device, but she outtops a hundred-odd patient attempts of fiction to sketch the pioneer wife. In her shrewdness, curiosity, initiative and brusque humanity one reads an entire history. Mere allusions—the ferryboat owner, the oarsmen who flee from smallpox, even raftsmen heard joking in the dark —have an incomparable authenticity. There is also the crowd. The loafers of Bricksville whittle under the store fronts. They set a dog upon a sow that has "wholloped" herself right down in the way and "laugh and look grateful for the noise." Presently a bubble rises through this human mire: the drunken Boggs, the best-naturedest old fool in Arkansaw, comes riding into Bricksville, on the waw-path. Colonel Sherburn finds it necessary to shoot him; and then, in one of the most blinding flashlights in all fiction, a "long, lanky man, with long hair and a big white fur stovepipe hat on the back of his head" rehearses the murder. "The people that had seen the thing said he done it perfect." So Buck Harkness leads a mob to Sherburn's house for a lynching but the Colonel breaks up the mob with a speech in which contempt effervesces like red nitric.

But in such passages as this, the clearly seen individuals merge into something greater, a social whole, a civilization, seen just as clearly. Pokeville, where the King is converted at the camp-meeting, Bricksville, and the town below the P'int where a tanner has died are one with Dawson's Landing and Napoleon—but more concentrated and thereby more final. It seems unnecessary to linger in consideration of this society. At the time of its appearance in 1885 a number of other novelists, perhaps fecundated by *The Gilded Age,* were considering similar themes. The name of any one of them—Charles Egbert Craddock or Mary E. Wilkins or Edward Eggleston will do—is enough to distinguish honest talent from genius. The impulse weakened under the æstheticism of the Nineties, and it was not till after the World War that the countryside again received consideration in these terms. To set Bricksville against Gopher Prairie or Winesburg is to perceive at once the finality of Mark Twain. The long lanky man in a white stovepipe hat who rehearses the death of Boggs has recorded this society with an unemotional certainty beside which either Mr. Lewis's anger or Mr. Anderson's misery seems a transitory hysterics.

The completeness of the society must be insisted upon. One should scrutinize the family of the dead tanner and their friends and neighbors, and orient them by reference to the family of Colonel Grangerford. The Wilkses belong to the industrious respectability of the towns. Their speech and thinking, the objects of their desire, the circumstances of their relationships are the totality of their kind. The funeral of Peter Wilks is, as fiction, many themes blended together; it is, among them, a supreme exhibition of the midcontinental culture of its time—almost an archæological display. When the undertaker tiptoes among the mourners to silence a howling dog and returns to whisper "He had a rat," something final has been said about this life. But Colonel Grangerford is a gentleman. Incidentally to the feud, which is the principal occupation of this episode, Southern gentility is examined. James's Basil Ransom was an embraced tradition; Colonel Grangerford is a reality. His daughter's elopement, a device for the precipitation of the plot, is out of fiction; the feud itself, with all the lovingly studied details of the scene, is from life. Gentility decorates the parlor with Emmeline Grangerford's verse and sketches. Its neurons show in the management of more than a hundred niggers quite as positively as in the parlor, or in the ceremonies of family intercourse and the simple code of honor, so indistinguishable from that of the Iroquois, which results in mass murder.

The portraiture which begins among the dregs with old man Finn ends with the Grangerfords. Between these strata has come every level of the South. What is the integrity of an artist? It would seem to consist in an intelligence which holds itself to the statement of a perceived truth, refusing to color it with an emotion of the artist's consequent to the truth. . . . These scenes are warm with an originality and a gusto that exist nowhere else in American fiction, and yet they are most notable for Mark Twain's detachment. There is no coloration, no resentment, no comment of any kind. The thing itself is rendered. If repudiation is complete, it exists implicitly in the thing.[2]

The differentiation of the speech these people use is so subtly done that Mark had to defend himself against an accusation of carelessness. He did not want readers to "suppose that all these characters were trying to talk alike and not succeeding." Superlatives are accurate once more: no equal sensitiveness to American speech has ever been brought to fiction. But a triumph in dialect is after all one of the smaller triumphs of novel-writing, and the important thing to be observed about Huckleberry's speech is its achievement in making the vernacular a perfect instrument for all the necessities of fiction. Like Melville, Mark Twain could write empty rhetoric enough when the mood was on him, and the set pieces of description in the travel books are as trying as the McGuffey selections which may have influenced them, while a willingness to let tears flow menaces a good many effects elsewhere. Yet his writing is never mediocre and is mostly, even in the least pretentious efforts, a formidable strength. Beginning with *Life on the Mississippi* it becomes, as Mr. Ford has remarked, one of the great styles of English literature. No analysis need be made here: its basis is simplicity, adaptability, an intimate liaison with the senses, and fidelity to the idioms of speech. Against the assertions of criticism, it should be remembered that such a style is not developed inattentively, nor are infants born with one by God's providence. Mark's lifelong pleasure in the peculiarities of language, which has distressed commentators, was the interest of any artist in his tools. . . . The successful use of an American vernacular as the sole prose medium of

2 Criticism has spent some pain on Mark Twain's deletion from *Life on the Mississippi* of a passage which, he was persuaded, might affect sales in the South. Apparently those who were outraged by this pandering to prejudice did not bother to read the suppressed passage. It is considerably less offensive to Southern sensibilities than several passages which remain in *Life on the Mississippi* and beside a good half of *Huckleberry Finn* it is innocuous.

a masterpiece is a triumph in technique. Such attempts have been common in two and a half centuries of English fiction, but no other attempt on the highest level has succeeded. In this respect, too, *Huckleberry Finn* is unique. Patently, American literature has nothing to compare with it. Huck's language is a sensitive, subtle, and versatile instrument—capable of every effect it is called upon to manage. Whether it be the purely descriptive necessity of recording the river's mystery, or the notation of psychological states so minute and transitory as the effect on a boy of ghosts crying in the wind, or the fixation of individuality in dialogue, or the charged finality that may be typified by the King's "Hain't we got all the fools in town on our side? And ain't that a big enough majority in any town?"—the prose fulfills its obligation with the casual competence of genius. The fiction of Mark Twain had brought many innovations to the national literature —themes, lives, and interests of the greatest originality. This superb adaptation of vernacular to the purposes of art is another innovation, one which has only in the last few years begun to have a dim and crude but still perceptible fruition.

A tradition almost as old as prose narrative joins to the novel another tributary of world literature when a purely American wandering brings two further creatures of twilight to the raft. The Duke of Bilgewater and the Lost Dauphin were born of Mark's inexhaustible delight in worthlessness, but are many-sided. Pretension of nobility is one of his commonest themes, here wrought into pure comedy. The Duke is akin to characters in the other books; the King embodies a legend widespread and unimaginably glorious on the frontier. The ambiguity surrounding the death of Louis XVII gave to history riots, dynasties and social comedies that still absorb much reverence in Florence and Paris. It gave mythology a superb legend, which at once accommodated itself to American belief. Up the river from New Orleans, one of the most pious repositories of allegiance, stories of the dethroned Bourbon gratified believers during three generations. The legend must have entertained Mark's boyhood but the circumstances of his Dauphin suggest that he more enjoyed the appearance of Eleazar Williams, who became an international celebrity in 1853. The whole course of his life probably gave him no more satisfying exhibition of the race's folly than the discovery of a Bourbon king in the person of this Mohawk half-breed turned Christian and missionary, who had systematically defrauded his church and his people. The story is one of the occasional ecstasies with which history rewards the patient mind.

The two rogues are formed from the nation's scum. They are products of chance and opportunity, drifters down rivers and across the countryside in the service of themselves. The Duke has sold medicines, among them a preparation to remove tartar from the teeth; he has acted tragedy and can sling a lecture sometimes; he can teach singing-geography school or take a turn to mesmerism or phrenology when there's a chance. The King can tell fortunes and can cure cancer or paralysis by the laying on of hands; but preaching, missionarying, and the temperance revival are his best lines. American universals meet here; once more, this is a whole history, and into these drifters is poured an enormous store of the nation's experience. They have begotten hordes of successors since 1885 but none that joins their immortality. They belong with Colonel Sellers: they are the pure stuff of comedy. Their destiny is guile: to collect the tax which freedom and wit levy on respectability. Their voyage is down a river deep in the American continent; they are born of a purely American scene. Yet the river becomes one of the world's roads and these disreputables join, of right, a select fellowship. They are Diana's foresters: the brotherhood that receives them, approving their passage, is immortal in the assenting dreams of literature. Such freed spirits as Panurge, Falstaff, Gil Blas and the Abbé Coignard are of that fellowship; no Americans except the Duke and the Dauphin have joined it. None seems likely to.

Yet the fabric on which all this richness is embroidered is the journey of Huck and Jim down the Mississippi on the June rise. There, finally, the book's glamour resides. To discuss that glamour would be futile. In a sense, Huck speaks to the national shrewdness, facing adequately what he meets, succeeding by means of native intelligence whose roots are ours—and ours only. In a sense, he exists for a delight or wonder inseparable from the American race. This passage down the flooded river, through pageantry and spectacle, amidst an infinite variety of life, something of surprise or gratification surely to be met with each new incident—it is the heritage of a nation not unjustly symbolized by the river's flow. Huck sleeping under the stars or wakefully drifting through an immensity dotted only by far lights or scurrying to a cave while the forest bends under a cloudburst satisfies blind gropings of the mind. The margin widens to obscurity. Beyond awareness, a need for freedom, an insatiable hunger for its use, finds in him a kind of satisfaction. At the margin, too, the endless flow speaks for something quite as immediate. It is movement, not quiet. By day or darkness the current is unceasing; its rhythm, at the obscure margin, speaks affirmatively. For life is movement—a down-river voyage amidst strangeness.

Go warily in that obscurity. One does not care to leave Huck in the twilight at such a threshold, among the dim shapes about which no one can speak with authority. Unquestionably something of him is resident there—with something of Tom, the disreputables, Colonel Sellers and some others. But first he is a shrewd boy who takes a raft down the Mississippi, through a world incomparably alive. With him goes a fullness made and shaped wholly of America. It is only because the world he passes through is real and only because it is American that his journey escapes into universals and is immortal. His book is American life formed into great fiction.

Somewhere in the person of Mark Twain, who wrote it, must have been an artist—as American.

Roads to Freedom

by Gladys Carmen Bellamy

It is no secret that Mark Twain had difficulty in writing *Huckleberry Finn*. He wrote about half of it and then put the manuscript away to gather dust for almost seven years; yet the finished whole seems easy, simple, natural. Huck, the unifying thread that ties everything together, gains in stature by having no taller rivals near him—only the river tramps who impose themselves on his generosity and the hunted Negro whom he befriends.

In spite of its episodic nature, the book falls naturally into three thematic units. In the first sixteen chapters the theme has to do with what is of and from St. Petersburg: Huck, Tom, Nigger Jim, and Pap. The second thematic unit includes the most strongly satiric, the most powerful part of the book, bringing Huck and Jim into contact with the outside world. In the cross-section of the South through which they journey, Huck witnesses the Grangerford-Shepherdson feud, the chicanery of the king and the duke, the killing of Boggs, Colonel Sherburn's quelling of the mob, and finally the village funeral. The characters of the king and the duke add to the thematic unity of this section. The third thematic unit is short, a sort of coda to the rest, covering the period at the Phelps farm in which Tom re-enters the story. This section repeats the romanticized motif of the first part and thus brings the book around full-circle, before its close.

The art of characterization is the one most important to a novelist, and Mark Twain's characters are his greatest literary achievement, Something of his method in characterization may be learned from a passage he wrote in 1907:

> Every man is in his own person the whole human race, with not a detail lacking. I am the whole human race without a detail lacking; I have studied the human race with diligence and strong interest all these years

in my own person; in myself I find in big or little proportion every quality and every defect that is findable in the mass of the race.

This suggests that when he had need of a certain trait, his habit was to dig for it within himself, to isolate and study it, then to enlarge it to the proportion proper to the character in question. This suggestion is borne out by a marginal note in one of his books: "If Byron—if any man—draws 50 characters, they are all himself—50 shades, 50 moods, of his own character. And when the man draws them well, why do they stir my admiration? Because they are me—I recognize myself."

A careful study of *Huckleberry Finn* shows that it is the characters and their interrelationship which determine the arrangement and structure of the book. The three thematic sections subdivide into little units notable for the contrast they offer each other. The first three chapters continue, naturally enough, the vein of *Tom Sawyer*, to which this book becomes a sort of sequel. Everything is colored by the excitement of Tom's imaginary adventures; he insists on doing all things according to the books he has read, from having his Gang sign in blood their oaths of allegiance to capturing and holding people for ransom. Ben Rogers, a Gang member, wants to know what being "ransomed" means, and Tom replies:

> "I don't know. But that's what they do. I've seen it in books; and of course that's what we've got to do."
> "But how can we do it if we don't know what it is?"
> "Why, blame it all, we've *got* to do it. Don't I tell you it's in the books? Do you want to go to doing different from what's in the books and get things all muddled up?"

And here, in a simple argument among boys, Mark Twain sets the pattern for this, his greatest story, as a satire on institutionalism. The three figures, Tom, Huck, and Jim, represent three gradations of thought and three levels of civilization. Tom, pretending so intensely that it becomes so, says we can't do it except as in the books. Is this what civilization really is—merely a pretense according to a set pattern? Tom is on the highest level, in the sense of being most civilized; but he represents a mawkish, romantic, artificial civilization. Compared with him, Nigger Jim and Huck are primitives; and the closer Mark Twain gets to primitivism, the better his writing becomes. He shows us the African in Jim, imbuing him with a dark knowledge that lies in his blood and his nerve ends. Huck Finn stands between these two; he is the "natural man," suggesting Walt Whitman's dream of the great American who should be simple and free. Both Tom and

Jim are in bondage to institutionalism.[1] Tom can't do anything against the rules of his books; Jim can't do anything against the rules of his taboos, his voodoo fears and charms and superstitions. Only Huck is free of institutions. Tom and Jim are always sure they are right, since each has his institution to consult and to follow; but Huck is tormented by doubts. When he is with Tom, he is willing to join Tom in following the books; when he is with Jim, he is careful not to break Jim's taboos, especially after the incident of the rattlesnake skin. But when Huck is alone, because he has no rules to go by he is guided by the voice within himself. He listens to what goes on inside him. He is free to probe within his own heart, where is to be found whatever bit of divinity man has—what we know as his soul.

If *Tom Sawyer* is accepted as a satire against the moralizing Sunday school tales, *Huckleberry Finn* has a much broader field as a satire against institutionalism in general. The institution of slavery is basic in this book, just as it is in *Pudd'nhead Wilson*. In *A Connecticut Yankee,* Mark Twain fulminates against church and state. In *Joan of Arc* he attacks the oppressions of formal religion and formal law. In *Hadleyburg* he frowns upon the institutionalism by which young people are trained in hypocrisy and the forms of empty "honor." Indeed, he sees the village itself as an institution—the tight little institution of the mores of the folk, which dictates the condemnation of all outlanders and innovators.

Within each of the thematic units in *Huckleberry Finn* there is a subtle variation of character and atmosphere. After the idyllic, romantic atmosphere which permeates the first three chapters, in the next four the story veers sharply from the mood of *Tom Sawyer,* and Pap takes the stage, drunken and disreputable, feeling himself the victim of sundry social ills. Into this satiric portrait went Mark Twain's years of observation of mountain whites, piney-woods people, and river rats. Pap is completely revealed through his oration on the "guv'ment." This unit ends when Huck flees because he fears his father will kill him in a fit of delirium tremens.

After so much violence, Jackson's Island gives him a feeling of peace. He explores the island, and just as he begins to feel lonely he discovers Jim, a Negro who has run away from home because his owner is planning to sell him "down to Orleans"—the Negro's equivalent of hell. Thereafter the runaway slave and the outcast waif share the island and comfort each other. This small unit of four chapters, the interlude on Jackson's Island, ends once more in the threat of violence and fear. Men are approaching the island to search for Jim.

[1] I am indebted to Professor Floyd Stovall for the suggestion that *Huckleberry Finn* is a satire on institutionalism, as well as for some suggestions pertaining to the structure of the book.

Mark Twain's prefatory note warns the reader that seven different dialects are used in the book; the shadings among them are so fine that not every reader can perceive them, and he does not want readers to think that "all these characters were trying to talk alike and not succeeding." His sensitivity to speech enabled him to say, "The shadings have not been done in haphazard fashion, or by guesswork, but painstakingly." But the artistry of such shadings in dialect fades before his skill in employing the vernacular of Huck Finn for a book-length narrative. Huck has a strong, vivid, natural imagination—not an artificial one, such as Tom's, or a superstitious one, such as Jim's. He describes, with memorable effect, a summer storm which he and Jim watched from the security of their cave on the island:

> . . . it looked all blue-black outside, and lovely; and the rain would thrash along by so thick that the trees off a little ways looked dim and spider-webby; and here would come a blast of wind that would bend the trees down and turn up the pale underside of the leaves; and then a perfect ripper of a gust would follow along and set the branches to tossing their arms as if they was just wild; and next, when it was just about the bluest and blackest—*fst!* it was as bright as glory, and you'd have a little glimpse of tree-tops a-plunging about away off yonder in the storm, hundreds of yards further than you could see before; dark as sin again in a second, and now you'd hear the thunder let go with an awful crash, and then go rumbling, grumbling, tumbling, down the sky towards the under side of the world, like rolling empty barrels down stairs—where it's long stairs and they bounce a good deal, you know.

Mark Twain's elemental imagination lends vigor and freshness to many passages. As Huck and Jim lie on their backs at night looking up at the stars, while the raft slips silently down the river, they argue about whether the stars "was made or only just happened": "Jim said the moon could 'a' *laid* them; well, that looked kind of reasonable . . . because I've seen a frog lay most as many." Huck describes Pap as having hair that was "long and tangled and greasy, and hung down, and you could see his eyes shining through like he was behind vines," while his face was white—"not like another man's white, but a white to make a body sick . . . a fish-belly white." At the parlor funeral of Peter Wilks, "the undertaker he slid around in his black gloves with his softy soothering ways, . . . making no more sound than a cat. . . . He was the softest, glidingest, stealthiest man I ever see." When the old king got a sudden shock, he "squshed down like a bluff bank that the river has cut under, it took him so sudden." Huck's language is equal to any effect demanded of it.

Part of the power of this book lies in Mark Twain's drawing of the character of Nigger Jim. From the time Jim first appears, a "big nigger" silhouetted in the kitchen door with the light behind him, he is a figure of dignity. In the famous syllogism in which Jim argues that since a Frenchman is a man, he should talk like a man, Mark Twain shows Jim's slow, purposeful reasoning. But in other moods Jim's spirit opens out to a wider horizon. Like Huck, he senses the beauty of the river. In his interpretation of a dream, Jim lets "the big, clear river" symbolize "the free States"—in other words, freedom. If "The Enchanted Village" might serve as a subtitle for *Tom Sawyer,* so "The Road to Freedom" might serve the same purpose for *Huckleberry Finn.* Jim has two big scenes in the book. One occurs when he relates the tragic moment of his discovery that his little girl was "plumb deef en dumb, Huck, plumb deef en dumb." His second big scene comes when he risks capture to help the doctor care for the wounded Tom Sawyer.

Whatever may be said of Tom Sawyer, Huck Finn is a developing character. Much of his development is due to his association with Jim and his increasing respect for the black man. In *Tom Sawyer,* Huck apologized to Tom for eating with a Negro, the Rogerses' Uncle Jake, who had given him food: "A body's got to do things when he's awful hungry he wouldn't . . . do as a steady thing." When he first finds Jim on the island, he is glad simply because he wants companionship; but as the two share the peace of the place, Huck comes to regard Jim as a human being rather than a faithful dog. When he hears there is a reward for Jim, the money offers no temptation to him; but under attack by his conscience, he fears he may have done wrong in helping a slave to escape. His traditions and environment pull him one way; what he feels in his heart pulls him the other way. Finally, he goes so far as to write a note to Miss Watson, Jim's owner, telling her where Jim is to be found. At first, he feels better for writing the note:

> . . . thinking how near I come to being lost and going to hell. . . . [Then I] got to thinking over our trip down the river; and I see Jim before me all the time: in the day and in the night-time, . . . and we a-floating along, talking and singing and laughing. But somehow I couldn't seem to strike no places to harden me against him, but only the other kind . . . and then I happened to look around and see that paper.
>
> It was a close place. I took it up and held it in my hand. I was a-trembling, because I'd got to decide, forever, betwixt two things, and I knowed it. I studied a minute, sort of holding my breath, and then says to myself: "All right, then, I'll *go* to hell"—and tore it up.

A part of Huck's development came when he apologized to Jim for fooling him about a dream. Jim very properly resented Huck's deceit, and Huck was abashed before Jim's stately indignation. When Huck waked in the night to find Jim mourning for his children—"Po' little 'Lizabeth! po' little Johnny!"—a new realization was borne in upon the boy: "I do believe he cared just as much for his people as white folks does for their'n. It don't seem natural, but I reckon it's so." Although the doctor and others seemed amazed at Jim's risking capture to aid the wounded Tom, Huck felt no surprise at all: "I knowed he was white inside."

The beautiful stretches of the river had power over Huck's spirit, as is shown in his own words: "It was kind of solemn, drifting down the big, still river . . . looking up at the stars, and we didn't ever feel like talking loud, and it warn't often we laughed." He has learned to read early in the story, and he reads at the Grangerford home; of *Pilgrim's Progress;* his verdict is, "The statements was interesting, but tough." He feels that somebody should write a poetical tribute to the dead Emmeline Grangerford, "so I tried to sweat out a verse or two myself, but I couldn't seem to make it go somehow." Such a sentiment would have seemed out of character for Huck in the beginning, but not now. He describes Colonel Grangerford as an aristocrat, and his own sensitive nature responds to the Colonel's fine-wire temperament: "everybody was always good-mannered where he was."

The first thematic unit ends with the smashing of the raft by a steamboat. This incident also ended the writing of *Huckleberry Finn* for almost seven years.[2] Mark Twain had written thus far in the summer of 1876; he apparently had no further plan, and when the raft was smashed, he stopped the book. Two years after he had shelved *Huckleberry Finn,* he wrote the 1878 letter to Howells, explaining that he felt himself unable to write successful satire because to do so calls for "a calm, judicial good humor." His trip down the river in 1882 to get material for *Life on the Mississippi* naturally recalled the river story to his mind. He must have then arrived at the design which made the book a masterpiece. All the meannesses of Mark Twain's "damned human race" are seen through the eyes and presented through the lips of Huck Finn. And thus Mark Twain was enabled, at last, to attain the calm detachment with which satire should be presented.

The second thematic unit begins when Huck stops at the Grangerford mansion after the wreck of the raft. The Grangerford-Shepherdson feud is one of the most tragic things in the book, but nothing is told with greater restraint. This restraint is art; but Mark Twain, as John Erskine observed, makes it seem the work of nature. Beginning his account of the climax of the feud, Huck says, "I don't want to

2 DeVoto, *Mark Twain at Work,* pp. 53, 62. [DeVoto's account of the composition of *Huckleberry Finn* has since been amended by Walter Blair's findings, summarized in the Introduction to this collection—ED.]

talk much about the next day." All that blood and dying was nau-
seating to the boy, and "it would make him sick again" if he should
tell about the killings. He tries not to remember the details, because
those memories spoil his sleep at night. To measure Mark Twain's
growth in artistry, one has only to compare this restraint with the
early sketches in which the reformer purposefully emphasized blood
and violence for their shock value in directing attention to situations
he deplored. Now, to get back to the raft and to Jim is, for Huck, like
going home; and his soul expands in the healing peace of the quiet
river: "We said there warn't no home like a raft. . . . Other places
do seem so cramped up and smothery."

After the episode of the feud, the king and the duke board the raft
and begin to dominate the lives of Huck and Jim. The loafers of
Bricksville, Arkansas, lean and whittle; around noon, they all laugh
and look glad, for old man Boggs comes riding into town drunk and
begins to blackguard Colonel Sherburn. Finally Sherburn's outraged
honor demands that he stop blackguarding with a bullet, and Boggs
dies in a little drugstore, with a heavy Bible on his chest.

All these wrongs are condemned through the mere fact of their
presentation. With the exception of one scene, Mark Twain is invisible, inaudible, lost in the artistry of Huck's particular kind of com-
munication. In that scene Colonel Sherburn appears on his veranda
to pour his withering scorn down upon the mob and send them scurrying like whipped curs. "I know you clear through. I was born and
raised in the South, and I've lived in the North." It is Mark Twain
speaking:

> So I know the average all around. The average man's a coward. . . .
> Your mistake is that you didn't bring a man with you; that's one mistake,
> and the other is that you didn't come in the dark and fetch your masks.
> . . . The pitifulest thing out is a mob . . . But a mob without any *man*
> at the head of it is *beneath* pitifulness. Now the thing for *you* to do is to
> droop your tails and go home and crawl in a hole.

Mark Twain's voice rings out, clear and unmistakable, in the hit at
militarism: "an army is—a mob; they don't fight with courage that's
born in them, but with courage that's borrowed from their mass."
If a "Colonel" had talked like that, would Huck have reported him
like that? No matter; the force of the book is so strong at this point
that the illusion is not shattered; but the utter objectivity of the scene
immediately preceding ranks it far above this one.

There, we see the innate cruelty of the dead-alive loafers. "There
couldn't anything wake them up all over, and make them happy all
over, like . . . putting turpentine on a stray dog and setting fire to

him, or tying a tin pan to his tail and see him run himself to death."
Then old Boggs rides in "on the waw-path," a pitiful figure who
"throwed his hat down in the mud and rode over it, and . . . went
a-raging down the street again, with his gray hair a-flying" while the
loafers, at first "listening and laughing and going on," are quickly
sobered by the ultimatum of Colonel Sherburn. "Everybody that seen
the shooting was telling how it happened," and one "long, lanky man,
with long hair and a big white fur stovepipe hat" enacted the scene
in its entirety. Huck's comment is, "The people that had seen the
thing said he done it perfect." And Mr. DeVoto adds that the long
lanky man records this society "with an unemotional certainty beside
which either Mr. Lewis's anger or Mr. Anderson's misery" seems merely
hysterical. Those who understand Mark Twain can only guess how
much of that calm detachment, that "unemotional certainty," was
sheer artistry, a triumph of technique.

With each of these scenes, Huck's character develops as his experience is widened. He perceives the manly qualities of Jim and scales
correctly the duke and the king; he knows that the duke is not so low
as the king, and yet he is tolerant of the "poor old king" when he sees
him in "a little low doggery, very tight, and a lot of loafers bullyrag-
ging him for sport." When Huck finds himself stranded on the *Walter
Scott* with some murderers, his sympathy, broad and beautiful, makes
him realize "how dreadful it was, even for murderers, to be in such
a fix. I says to myself, there ain't no telling but I might come to be
a murderer myself yet, and then how would I like it?" In his last
glimpse of the king and the duke, tarred and feathered so that they
"just looked like a couple of monstrous big soldier-plumes," he was
"sorry for them poor pitiful rascals," and it made him sick to see it:
"Human beings *can* be awful cruel to one another."

There is an occasional hint of determinism in *Huckleberry Finn*.
Early in the story Huck backslides under the power of environment
while living with Pap: ". . . I was used to being where I was, and
liked it." If fear of his drunken father had not driven him forth,
Mark Twain seems to say, Huck might have become another Pap.
When his conscience troubles him over not giving up the runaway
slave, he excuses himself on the ground of early environment and its
effects:

> . . . I knowed very well I had done wrong, and I see it warn't no use for
> me to try to learn to do right; a body that don't get *started* right when
> he's little ain't got no show—when the pinch comes there ain't nothing
> to back him up. . . . Then I . . . says to myself, hold on; s'pose you'd a
> done right and give Jim up, would you felt better than what you do now?
> No, I says, I'd feel bad—I'd feel just the same way I do now. Well, then,

says I, what's the use you learning to do right when it's troublesome to do right and ain't no trouble to do wrong, and the wages is the same?

Huck's questioning of himself recalls Ernest Hemingway's definition of morality, which appears early in *Death in the Afternoon:* "I know only that what is moral is what you feel good after." Unquestionably, Mark Twain and Hemingway are akin in their preoccupation with death and in the care and skill with which they write the idiom of their people; but it seems to me that Hemingway's nearest approach to the earlier writer lies in the moral tests his characters apply inwardly. Having no moral code to go by, they test an action by the way they feel after it.[3]

Huck usually looks into his own heart for guidance. He "goes to studying things out" whenever he feels himself "in a tight place." He learns from experience, but his environment determines him only as his experiences develop what is within. Moral intuition is the basis on which his character rests. But if a man is not responsible to God or to society, and Mark Twain's determinism holds that he is not, why should he be responsible to himself? The inner voice of conscience, the voice of God, always holds him morally responsible. In this way *Huckleberry Finn* is a wise book, as all great books are wise.

*   *   *

Huck wins his battle with his "yaller dog" conscience and continues, Mr. DeVoto observes, to vindicate "the realities of friendship, loyalty, and courage." DeVoto doubts that Mark Twain could have asserted them except in the belief of a boy. Perhaps it was, in part, the comparatively keen consciences of the young that attracted him. Like Hawthorne, he accepted the dramatic reality of the issues of conscience; Huck's conscience becomes the battleground for the chief struggle of the book. Although not dissatisfied with life, Huck is sometimes briefly pessimistic, as when he predicts that his Pap has likely "got [the money] all away from Judge Thatcher and drunk it up." But this prediction does not leave him despondent—he is ready to accept life as it comes. And Mr. DeVoto insists that "if the book makes a statement through Nigger Jim that human life is tragic, it also asserts through Huck that human life is noble . . . noble enough for the likes of us. . . . It is not a book of despair but rather of realistic acceptance."

[3] Joseph Warren Beach said, "In certain ways, contemporary American fiction opens with Ernest Hemingway." In the first chapter of *Green Hills of Africa,* Hemingway himself said: "All modern American literature comes from one book by Mark Twain called *Huckleberry Finn.* . . . it's the best book we've had. All American writing comes from that. There was nothing before. There has been nothing as good since."

It is chiefly in his boy-books, however, that Mark Twain was able to achieve this "realistic acceptance," this synthesis of both aspects of life. The joint charge of Brooks and DeVoto that he was imprisoned in his boyhood is thus seen to have supporting evidence. But the reason for that apparent imprisonment is also plain: Mark Twain was artist enough to know—or to sense, unconsciously, if you will—that such a synthesis, such a realistic acceptance, is demanded by the very nature of art. And so he turned again and again to the boy-world, the place where he could best achieve that synthesis and achieve it honestly. For he was honest; and he could rarely bring himself to an acceptance of human nature as exemplified in adults.

Mr. Eliot, Mr. Trilling, and *Huckleberry Finn*

by Leo Marx

In the losing battle that the plot fights with the characters, it often takes a cowardly revenge. Nearly all novels are feeble at the end. This is because the plot requires to be wound up. Why is this necessary? Why is there not a convention which allows a novelist to stop as soon as he feels muddled or bored? Alas, he has to round things off, and usually the characters go dead while he is at work, and our final impression of them is through deadness.

—E. M. FORSTER

The Adventures of Huckleberry Finn has not always occupied its present high place in the canon of American literature. When it was first published in 1885, the book disturbed and offended many reviewers, particularly spokesmen for the genteel tradition.[1] In fact, a fairly accurate inventory of the narrow standards of such critics might be made simply by listing epithets they applied to Clemens' novel. They called it vulgar, rough, inelegant, irreverent, coarse, semi-obscene, trashy and vicious.[2] So much for them. Today (we like to think) we know the true worth of the book. Everyone now agrees that *Huckleberry Finn* is a masterpiece: it is probably the one book in our literature about which highbrows and lowbrows can agree. Our most serious critics praise it. Nevertheless, a close look at what two of the best

---

"*Mr. Eliot, Mr. Trilling, and* Huckleberry Finn" *by Leo Marx. From* The American Scholar, *XXII (Autumn, 1953), 423-40. Copyright © 1953 by the United Chapters of Phi Beta Kappa. Reprinted by permission of author and publisher.*

[1] I use the term "genteel tradition" as George Santayana characterized it in his famous address "The Genteel Tradition in American Philosophy," first delivered in 1911 and published the following year in his *Winds of Doctrine.* Santayana described the genteel tradition as an "old mentality" inherited from Europe. It consists of the various dilutions of Christian theology and morality, as in transcendentalism—a fastidious and stale philosophy of life no longer relevant to the thought and activities of the United States. "America," he said, "is a young country with an old mentality." (Later references to Santayana also refer to this essay.)

[2] For an account of the first reviews, see A. L. Vogelback, "The Publication and Reception of *Huckleberry Finn* in America," *American Literature,* XI (November, 1939), 260-72.

among them have recently written will likewise reveal, I believe, serious weaknesses in current criticism. Today the problem of evaluating the book is as much obscured by unqualified praise as it once was by parochial hostility.

I have in mind essays by Lionel Trilling and T. S. Eliot.[3] Both praise the book, but in praising it both feel obligated to say something in justification of what so many readers have felt to be its great flaw: the disappointing "ending," the episode which begins when Huck arrives at the Phelps place and Tom Sawyer reappears. There are good reasons why Mr. Trilling and Mr. Eliot should feel the need to face this issue. From the point of view of scope alone, more is involved than the mere "ending"; the episode comprises almost one-fifth of the text. The problem, in any case, is unavoidable. I have discussed *Huckleberry Finn* in courses with hundreds of college students, and I have found only a handful who did not confess their dissatisfaction with the extravagant mock rescue of Nigger Jim and the denouement itself. The same question always comes up: "What went wrong with Twain's novel?" Even Bernard DeVoto, whose wholehearted commitment to Clemens' genius is well known, has said of the ending that "in the whole reach of the English novel there is no more abrupt or more chilling descent." [4] Mr. Trilling and Mr. Eliot do not agree. They both attempt, and on similar grounds, to explain and defend the conclusion.

Of the two, Mr. Trilling makes the more moderate claim for Clemens' novel. He does admit that there is a "falling off" at the end; nevertheless he supports the episode as having "a certain formal aptness." Mr. Eliot's approval is without serious qualification. He allows no objections, asserts that "it is right that the mood of the end of the book should bring us back to the beginning." I mean later to discuss their views in some detail, but here it is only necessary to note that both critics see the problem as one of form. And so it is. Like many questions of form in literature, however, this one is not finally separable from a question of "content," of value, or, if you will, of moral insight. To bring *Huckleberry Finn* to a satisfactory close, Clemens had to do more than find a neat device for ending a story. His problem, though it may never have occurred to him, was to invent an action capable of placing in focus the meaning of the journey down the Mississippi.

I believe that the ending of *Huckleberry Finn* makes so many readers uneasy because they rightly sense that it jeopardizes the significance

3 Mr. Eliot's essay is the introduction to the edition of *Huckleberry Finn* published by Chanticleer Press, New York, 1950. Mr. Trilling's is the introduction to an edition of the novel published by Rinehart, New York, 1948, and later reprinted in his *The Liberal Imagination*, Viking, New York, 1950.

4 *Mark Twain at Work* (Cambridge, 1942), p. 92.

of the entire novel. To take seriously what happens at the Phelps farm
is to take lightly the entire downstream journey. What is the meaning
of the journey? With this question all discussion of *Huckleberry Finn*
must begin. It is true that the voyage down the river has many aspects
of a boy's idyl. We owe much of its hold upon our imagination to the
enchanting image of the raft's unhurried drift with the current. The
leisure, the absence of constraint, the beauty of the river—all these
things delight us. "It's lovely to live on a raft." And the multitudinous
life of the great valley we see through Huck's eyes has a fascination of
its own. Then, of course, there is humor—laughter so spontaneous, so
free of the bitterness present almost everywhere in American humor
that readers often forget how grim a spectacle of human existence Huck
contemplates. Humor in this novel flows from a bright joy of life as
remote from our world as living on a raft.

Yet along with the idyllic and the epical and the funny in *Huckleberry Finn,* there is a coil of meaning which does for the disparate
elements of the novel what a spring does for a watch. The meaning is
not in the least obscure. It is made explicit again and again. The very
words with which Clemens launches Huck and Jim upon their voyage
indicate that theirs is not a boy's lark but a quest for freedom. From
the electrifying moment when Huck comes back to Jackson's Island
and rouses Jim with the news that a search party is on the way, we are
meant to believe that Huck is enlisted in the cause of freedom. "Git
up and hump yourself, Jim!" he cries. "There ain't a minute to lose.
They're after us!" What particularly counts here is the *us.* No one is
after Huck; no one but Jim knows he is alive. In that small word
Clemens compresses the exhilarating power of Huck's instinctive humanity. His unpremeditated identification with Jim's flight from slavery is an unforgettable moment in American experience, and it may
be said at once that any culmination of the journey which detracts
from the urgency and dignity with which it begins will necessarily be
unsatisfactory. Huck realizes this himself, and says so when, much
later, he comes back to the raft after discovering that the Duke and the
King have sold Jim:

> After all this long journey . . . here it was all come to nothing, every-
> thing all busted up and ruined, because they could have the heart to
> serve Jim such a trick as that, and make him a slave again all his life,
> and amongst strangers, too, for forty dirty dollars.

Huck knows that the journey will have been a failure unless it takes
Jim to freedom. It is true that we do discover, in the end, that Jim
is free, but we also find out that the journey was not the means by
which he finally reached freedom.

The most obvious thing wrong with the ending, then, is the flimsy contrivance by which Clemens frees Jim. In the end we not only discover that Jim has been a free man for two months, but that his freedom has been granted by old Miss Watson. If this were only a mechanical device for terminating the action, it might not call for much comment. But it is more than that: it is a significant clue to the import of the last ten chapters. Remember who Miss Watson is. She is the Widow's sister whom Huck introduces in the first pages of the novel. It is she who keeps "pecking" at Huck, who tries to teach him to spell and to pray and to keep his feet off the furniture. She is an ardent proselytizer for piety and good manners, and her greed provides the occasion for the journey in the first place. She is Jim's owner, and he decides to flee only when he realizes that she is about to break her word (she cannot resist a slave trader's offer of eight hundred dollars) and sell him down the river away from his family.

Miss Watson, in short, is the Enemy. If we except a predilection for physical violence, she exhibits all the outstanding traits of the valley society. She pronounces the polite lies of civilization that suffocate Huck's spirit. The freedom which Jim seeks, and which Huck and Jim temporarily enjoy aboard the raft, is accordingly freedom *from* everything for which Miss Watson stands. Indeed, the very intensity of the novel derives from the discordance between the aspirations of the fugitives and the respectable code for which she is a spokesman. Therefore, her regeneration, of which the deathbed freeing of Jim is the unconvincing sign, hints a resolution of the novel's essential conflict. Perhaps because this device most transparently reveals that shift in point of view which he could not avoid, and which is less easily discerned elsewhere in the concluding chapters, Clemens plays it down. He makes little attempt to account for Miss Watson's change of heart, a change particularly surprising in view of Jim's brazen escape. Had Clemens given this episode dramatic emphasis appropriate to its function, Miss Watson's bestowal of freedom upon Jim would have proclaimed what the rest of the ending actually accomplishes—a vindication of persons and attitudes Huck and Jim had symbolically repudiated when they set forth downstream.

It may be said, and with some justice, that a reading of the ending as a virtual reversal of meanings implicit in the rest of the novel misses the point—that I have taken the final episode too seriously. I agree that Clemens certainly did not intend us to read it so solemnly. The ending, one might contend, is simply a burlesque upon Tom's taste for literary romance. Surely the tone of the episode is familiar to readers of Mark Twain. The preposterous monkey business attendant upon Jim's "rescue," the careless improvisation, the nonchalant disregard for common-sense plausibility—all these things should not surprise readers of Twain or any low comedy in the tradition of "Western humor." However, the trouble is, first, that the ending hardly comes off as burlesque: it is *too* fanciful, *too* extravagant; and it is tedious. For example, to provide a "gaudy" atmosphere for the escape, Huck and Tom catch a couple of dozen snakes. Then the snakes escape.

> No, there warn't no real scarcity of snakes about the house for a considerable spell. You'd see them dripping from the rafters and places every now and then; and they generly landed in your plate, or down the back of your neck . . .

Even if this were *good* burlesque, which it is not, what is it doing here? It is out of keeping; the slapstick tone jars with the underlying seriousness of the voyage.

Huckleberry Finn is a masterpiece because it brings Western humor to perfection and yet transcends the narrow limits of its conventions. But the ending does not. During the final extravaganza we are forced to put aside many of the mature emotions evoked earlier by the vivid rendering of Jim's fear of capture, the tenderness of Huck's and Jim's regard for each other, and Huck's excruciating moments of wavering between honesty and respectability. None of these emotions are called forth by the anticlimactic final sequence. I do not mean to suggest that the inclusion of low comedy per se is a flaw in *Huckleberry Finn*. One does not object to the shenanigans of the rogues; there is ample precedent for the place of extravagant humor even in works of high seriousness. But here the case differs from most which come to mind: the major characters themselves are forced to play low comedy roles. Moreover, the most serious motive in the novel, Jim's yearning for freedom, is made the object of nonsense. The conclusion, in short, is farce, but the rest of the novel is not.

That Clemens reverts in the end to the conventional manner of Western low comedy is most evident in what happens to the principals. Huck and Jim become comic characters; that is a much more serious ground for dissatisfaction than the unexplained regeneration of Miss Watson. Remember that Huck has grown in stature throughout the journey. By the time he arrives at the Phelps place, he is not the boy who had been playing robbers with Tom's gang in St. Petersburg the summer before. All he had seen and felt since he parted from Tom has deepened his knowledge of human nature and of himself. Clemens makes a point of Huck's development in two scenes which occur just before he meets Tom again. The first describes Huck's final capitulation to his own sense of right and wrong: "All right, then, I'll *go* to Hell." This is the climactic moment in the ripening of his self-knowledge. Shortly afterward, when he comes upon a mob riding the Duke and the King out of town on a rail, we are given his most memorable insight into the nature of man. Although these rogues had subjected Huck to every indignity, what he sees provokes this cele-brated comment:

> Well, it made me sick to see it; and I was sorry for them poor pitiful rascals, it seemed like I couldn't ever feel any hardness against them any more in the world. It was a dreadful thing to see. Human beings *can* be awful cruel to one another.

The sign of Huck's maturity here is neither the compassion nor the skepticism, for both had been marks of his personality from the first. Rather, the special quality of these reflections is the extraordinary com-bination of the two, a mature blending of his instinctive suspicion of human motives with his capacity for pity.

But at this point Tom reappears. Soon Huck has fallen almost com-pletely under his sway once more, and we are asked to believe that the boy who felt pity for the rogues is now capable of making Jim's cap-ture the occasion for a game. He becomes Tom's helpless accomplice, submissive and gullible. No wonder that Clemens has Huck remark, when Huck first realizes Aunt Sally has mistaken him for Tom, that "it was like being born again." Exactly. In the end, Huck regresses to the subordinate role in which he had first appeared in *The Adventures of Tom Sawyer*. Most of those traits which made him so appealing a hero now disappear. He had never, for example, found pain or misfor-tune amusing. At the circus, when a clown disguised as a drunk took a precarious ride on a prancing horse, the crowd loved the excitement and danger; "it warn't funny to me, though," said Huck. But now, in the end, he submits in awe to Tom's notion of what is amusing. To satisfy Tom's hunger for adventure he makes himself a party to sport which aggravates Jim's misery.

It should be added at once that Jim doesn't mind too much. The fact is that he has undergone a similar transformation. On the raft he was an individual, man enough to denounce Huck when Huck made him the victim of a practical joke. In the closing episode, however, we lose sight of Jim in the maze of farcical invention. He ceases to be a man. He allows Huck and "Mars Tom" to fill his hut with rats and snakes, "and every time a rat bit Jim he would get up and write a line in his journal whilst the ink was fresh." This creature who bleeds ink and feels no pain is something less than human. He has been made over in the image of a flat stereotype: the submissive stage-Negro. These antics divest Jim, as well as Huck, of much of his dignity and individuality.[5]

5 For these observations on the transformation of Jim in the closing episodes, I am indebted to the excellent unpublished essay by Mr. Chadwick Hansen on the subject of Clemens and Western humor [subsequently published as "The Character of Jim and the Ending of *Huckleberry Finn*," *Massachusetts Review*, V (Autumn, 1963), 45-66—ED.].

What I have been saying is that the flimsy devices of plot, the discordant farcical tone, and the disintegration of the major characters all betray the failure of the ending. These are not aspects merely of form in a technical sense, but of meaning. For that matter, I would maintain that this book has little or no formal unity independent of the joint purpose of Huck and Jim. What components of the novel, we may ask, provide the continuity which links one adventure with another? The most important is the unifying consciousness of Huck, the narrator, and the fact that we follow the same principals through the entire string of adventures. Events, moreover, occur in a temporal sequence. Then there is the river; after each adventure Huck and Jim return to the raft and the river. Both Mr. Trilling and Mr. Eliot speak eloquently of the river as a source of unity, and they refer to the river as a god. Mr. Trilling says that Huck is "the servant of the river-god." Mr. Eliot puts it this way: "The River gives the book its form. But for the River, the book might be only a sequence of adventures with a happy ending." This seems to me an extravagant view of the function of the neutral agency of the river. Clemens had a knowledgeable respect for the Mississippi, and, without sanctifying it, was able to provide excellent reasons for Huck's and Jim's intense relation with it. It is a source of food and beauty and terror and serenity of mind. But above all, it provides motion; it is the means by which Huck and Jim move away from a menacing civilization. They return to the river to continue their journey. The river cannot, does not, supply purpose. That purpose is a facet of their consciousness, and without the motive of escape from society, *Huckleberry Finn* would indeed "be only a sequence of adventures." Mr. Eliot's remark indicates how lightly he takes the quest for freedom. His somewhat fanciful exaggeration of the river's role is of a piece with his neglect of the theme at the novel's center.

That theme is heightened by the juxtaposition of sharp images of contrasting social orders: the microcosmic community Huck and Jim establish aboard the raft and the actual society which exists along the Mississippi's banks. The two are separated by the river, the road to freedom upon which Huck and Jim must travel. Huck tells us what the river means to them when, after the Wilks episode, he and Jim once again shove their raft into the current: "It *did* seem so good to be free again and all by ourselves on the big river, and nobody to bother us." The river is indifferent. But its sphere is relatively uncontaminated by the civilization they flee, and so the river allows Huck and Jim some measure of freedom at once, the moment they set foot on Jackson's Island or the raft. Only on the island and the raft do they have a chance to practice that idea of brotherhood to which they are devoted. "Other places do seem so cramped up and smothery," Huck explains, "but a raft don't. You feel mighty free and easy and comfortable on a raft." The main thing is freedom.

On the raft the escaped slave and the white boy try to practice their code: "What you want, above all things, on a raft, is for everybody to be satisfied, and feel right and kind towards the others." This human credo constitutes the paramount affirmation of *The Adventures of Huckleberry Finn,* and it obliquely aims a devastating criticism at the existing social order. It is a creed which Huck and Jim bring to the river. It neither emanates from nature nor is it addressed to nature. Therefore I do not see that it means much to talk about the river as a god in this novel. The river's connection with this high aspiration for man is that it provides a means of escape, a place where the code can be tested. The truly profound meanings of the novel are generated by the impingement of the actual world of slavery, feuds, lynching, murder, and a spurious Christian morality upon the ideal of the raft. The result is a tension which somehow demands release in the novel's ending.

But Clemens was unable to effect this release and at the same time control the central theme. The unhappy truth about the ending of *Huckleberry Finn* is that the author, having revealed the tawdry nature of the culture of the great valley, yielded to its essential complacency. The general tenor of the closing scenes, to which the token regeneration of Miss Watson is merely one superficial clue, amounts to just that. In fact, this entire reading of *Huckleberry Finn* merely confirms the brilliant insight of George Santayana, who many years ago spoke of American humorists, of whom he considered Mark Twain an outstanding representative, as having only "half escaped" the genteel tradition. Santayana meant that men like Clemens were able to "point to what contradicts it in the facts; but not in order to abandon the genteel tradition, for they have nothing solid to put in its place." This seems to me the real key to the failure of *Huckleberry Finn.* Clemens had presented the contrast between the two social orders but could not, or would not, accept the tragic fact that the one he had rejected was an image of solid reality and the other an ecstatic dream. Instead he gives us the cozy reunion with Aunt Polly in a scene fairly bursting with approbation of the entire family, the Phelpses included.

Like Miss Watson, the Phelpses are almost perfect specimens of the dominant culture. They are kind to their friends and relatives; they have no taste for violence; they are people capable of devoting themselves to their spectacular dinners while they keep Jim locked in the little hut down by the ash hopper, with its lone window boarded up. (Of course Aunt Sally visits Jim to see if he is "comfortable," and Uncle Silas comes in "to pray with him.") These people, with their comfortable Sunday-dinner conviviality and the runaway slave padlocked nearby, are reminiscent of those solid German citizens we have heard about in our time who tried to maintain a similarly *gemütlich* way of life within virtual earshot of Buchenwald. I do not mean to imply that Clemens was unaware of the shabby morality of such people. After the abortive escape of Jim, when Tom asks about him, Aunt Sally replies: "Him? . . . the runaway nigger? . . . They've got him back, safe and sound, and he's in the cabin again, on bread and water, and loaded down with chains, till he's claimed or sold!" Clemens understood people like the Phelpses, but nevertheless he was forced to rely upon them to provide his happy ending. The satisfactory outcome of Jim's quest for freedom must be attributed to the benevolence of the very people whose inhumanity first made it necessary.

But to return to the contention of Mr. Trilling and Mr. Eliot that the ending is more or less satisfactory after all. As I have said, Mr. Trilling approves of the "formal aptness" of the conclusion. He says that "some device is needed to permit Huck to return to his anonymity, to give up the role of hero," and that therefore "nothing could serve better than the mind of Tom Sawyer with its literary furnishings, its conscious romantic desire for experience and the hero's part, and its ingenious schematization of life. . . ." Though more detailed, this is essentially akin to Mr. Eliot's blunt assertion that "it is right that the mood at the end of the book should bring us back to that of the beginning." I submit that it is wrong for the end of the book to bring us back to that mood. The mood of the beginning of *Huckleberry Finn* is the mood of Huck's attempt to accommodate himself to the ways of St. Petersburg. It is the mood of the end of *The Adventures of Tom Sawyer,* when the boys had been acclaimed heroes, and when Huck was accepted as a candidate for respectability. That is the state in which we find him at the beginning of *Huckleberry Finn.* But Huck cannot stand the new way of life, and his mood gradually shifts to the mood of rebellion which dominates the novel until he meets Tom again. At first, in the second chapter, we see him still eager to be accepted by the nice boys of the town. Tom leads the gang in re-enacting adventures he has culled from books, but gradually Huck's pragmatic turn of mind gets him in trouble. He has little tolerance for Tom's brand of make-believe. He irritates Tom. Tom calls him a "numbskull," and finally Huck throws up the whole business:

> So then I judged that all that stuff was only just one of Tom Sawyer's lies. I reckoned he believed in the A-rabs and the elephants, but as for me I think different. It had all the marks of a Sunday-school.

With this statement, which ends the third chapter, Huck parts company with Tom. The fact is that Huck has rejected Tom's romanticizing of experience; moreover, he has rejected it as part of the larger pattern of society's make-believe, typified by Sunday school. But if he cannot accept Tom's harmless fantasies about the A-rabs, how are we to believe that a year later Huck is capable of awe-struck submission to the far more extravagant fantasies with which Tom invests the mock rescue of Jim?

After Huck's escape from his "pap," the drift of the action, like that of the Mississippi's current, is *away* from St. Petersburg. Huck leaves Tom and the A-rabs behind, along with the Widow, Miss Watson, and all the pseudo-religious ritual in which nice boys must partake. The return, in the end, to the mood of the beginning therefore means defeat—Huck's defeat; to return to that mood *joyously* is to portray defeat in the guise of victory.

Mr. Eliot and Mr. Trilling deny this. The overriding consideration for them is form—form which seems largely to mean symmetry of structure. It is fitting, Mr. Eliot maintains, that the book should come full circle and bring Huck once more under Tom's sway. Why? Because it begins that way. But it seems to me that such structural unity is *imposed* upon the novel, and thefore is meretricious. It is a jerry-built structure, achieved only by sacrifice of characters and theme. Here the controlling principle of form apparently is unity, but unfortunately a unity much too superficially conceived. Structure, after all, is only one element—indeed, one of the more mechanical elements—of unity. A unified work must surely manifest coherence of meaning and clear development of theme, yet the ending of *Huckleberry Finn* blurs both. The eagerness of Mr. Eliot and Mr. Trilling to justify the ending is symptomatic of that absolutist impulse of our critics to find reasons, once a work has been admitted to the highest canon of literary reputability, for admiring every bit of it.

What is perhaps most striking about these judgments of Mr. Eliot's and Mr. Trilling's is that they are so patently out of harmony with the basic standards of both critics. For one thing, both men hold far more complex ideas of the nature of literary unity than their comments upon *Huckleberry Finn* would suggest. For another, both critics are essentially moralists, yet here we find them turning away from a moral issue in order to praise a dubious structural unity. Their efforts to explain away the flaw in Clemens' novel suffer from a certain narrowness surprising to anyone who knows their work. These facts suggest that we may be in the presence of a tendency in contemporary criticism which the critics themselves do not fully recognize.

Is there an explanation? How does it happen that two of our most respected critics should seem to treat so lightly the glaring lapse of moral imagination in *Huckleberry Finn*? Perhaps—and I stress the conjectural nature of what I am saying—perhaps the kind of moral issue raised by *Huckleberry Finn* is not the kind of moral issue to which to-day's criticism readily addresses itself. Today our critics, no less than our novelists and poets, are most sensitively attuned to moral problems which arise in the sphere of individual behavior. They are deeply aware of sin, of individual infractions of our culture's Christian ethic. But my impression is that they are, possibly because of the strength of the reaction against the mechanical sociological criticism of the thirties, less sensitive to questions of what might be called social or political morality.

By social or political morality I refer to the values implicit in a social system, values which may be quite distinct from the personal morality of any given individual within the society. Now *The Adventures of Huckleberry Finn*, like all novels, deals with the behavior of individuals. But one mark of Clemens' greatness is his deft presentation of the disparity between what people do when they behave as individuals and what they do when forced into roles imposed upon them by society. Take, for example, Aunt Sally and Uncle Silas Phelps, who consider themselves Christians, who are by impulse generous and humane, but who happen also to be staunch upholders of certain degrading and inhuman social institutions. When they are confronted with an escaped slave, the imperatives of social morality outweigh all pious professions.

The conflict between what people think they stand for and what social pressure forces them to do is central to the novel. It is present to the mind of Huck and, indeed, accounts for his most serious inner conflicts. He knows how he feels about Jim, but he also knows what he is expected to do about Jim. This division within his mind corresponds to the division of the novel's moral terrain into the areas represented by the raft on the one hand and society on the other. His victory over his "yaller dog" conscience therefore assumes heroic size: it is a victory over the prevailing morality. But the last fifth of the novel has the effect of diminishing the importance and uniqueness of Huck's victory. We are asked to assume that somehow freedom can be achieved in spite of the crippling power of what I have called the social morality. Consequently the less importance we attach to that force as it operates in the novel, the more acceptable the ending becomes.

Moreover, the idea of freedom, which Mr. Eliot and Mr. Trilling seem to slight, takes on its full significance only when we acknowledge the power which society exerts over the minds of men in the world of *Huckleberry Finn*. For freedom in this book specifically means freedom from society and its imperatives. This is not the traditional Christian conception of freedom. Huck and Jim seek freedom not from a burden of individual guilt and sin, but from social constraint. That is to say, evil in *Huckleberry Finn* is the product of civilization, and if this is indicative of Clemens' rather too simple view of human nature, nevertheless the fact is that Huck, when he can divest himself of the taint of social conditioning (as in the incantatory account of sunrise on the river), is entirely free of anxiety and guilt. The only guilt he actually knows arises from infractions of a social code. (The guilt he feels after playing the prank on Jim stems from his betrayal of the law of the raft.) Huck's and Jim's creed is secular. Its object is harmony among men, and so Huck is not much concerned with his own salvation. He repeatedly renounces prayer in favor of pragmatic solutions to his problems. In other words, the central insights of the novel belong to the tradition of the Enlightenment. The meaning of the quest itself is hardly reconcilable with that conception of human nature embodied in the myth of original sin. In view of the current fashion of reaffirming man's innate depravity, it is perhaps not surprising to find the virtues of *Huckleberry Finn* attributed not to its meaning but to its form.

But "if this was not the right ending for the book," Mr. Eliot asks, "what ending would have been right?" Although this question places the critic in an awkward position (he is not always equipped to rewrite what he criticizes), there are some things which may justifiably be said about the "right" ending of *Huckleberry Finn*. It may be legitimate, even if presumptuous, to indicate certain conditions which a hypothetical ending would have to satisfy if it were to be congruent with the rest of the novel. If the conclusion is not to be something merely tacked on to close the action, then its broad outline must be immanent in the body of the work.

It is surely reasonable to ask that the conclusion provide a plausible outcome to the quest. Yet freedom, in the ecstatic sense that Huck and Jim knew it aboard the raft, was hardly to be had in the Mississippi Valley in the 1840's, or, for that matter, in any other known human society. A satisfactory ending would inevitably cause the reader some frustration. That Clemens felt such disappointment to be inevitable is borne out by an examination of the novel's clear, if unconscious, symbolic pattern. Consider, for instance, the inferences to be drawn from the book's geography. The river, to whose current Huck and Jim entrust themselves, actually carries them to the heart of slave territory. Once the raft passes Cairo, the quest is virtually doomed. Until the steamboat smashes the raft, we are kept in a state of anxiety about Jim's escape. (It may be significant that at this point Clemens found himself unable to continue work on the manuscript, and put it aside for several years.) Beyond Cairo, Clemens allows the intensity of that anxiety to diminish, and it is probably no accident that the fainter it becomes, the more he falls back upon the devices of low comedy. Huck and Jim make no serious effort to turn north, and there are times (during the Wilks episode) when Clemens allows Huck to forget all about Jim. It is as if the author, anticipating the dilemma he had finally to face, instinctively dissipated the power of his major theme.

Consider, too, the circumscribed nature of the raft as a means of moving toward freedom. The raft lacks power and maneuverability. It can only move easily with the current—southward into slave country. Nor can it evade the mechanized power of the steamboat. These impotencies of the raft correspond to the innocent helplessness of its occupants. Unresisted, the rogues invade and take over the raft. Though it is the symbolic locus of the novel's central affirmations, the raft provides an uncertain and indeed precarious mode of traveling toward freedom. This seems another confirmation of Santayana's perception. To say that Clemens only half escaped the genteel tradition is not to say that he failed to note any of the creed's inadequacies, but rather that he had "nothing solid" to put in its place. The raft patently was not capable of carrying the burden of hope Clemens placed upon it.[6] (Whether this is to be attributed to the nature of his vision or to the actual state of American society in the nineteenth century is another interesting question.) In any case, the geography of the novel, the raft's powerlessness, the goodness and vulnerability of Huck and Jim, all prefigure a conclusion quite different in tone from that which Clemens gave us. These facts constitute what Hart Crane might have called the novel's "logic of metaphor," and this logic—probably inadvertent—actually takes us to the underlying meaning of *The Adventures of Huckleberry Finn.* Through the symbols we reach a truth which the ending obscures: the quest cannot succeed.

Fortunately, Clemens broke through to this truth in the novel's last sentences:

> But I reckon I got to light out for the territory ahead of the rest, because Aunt Sally she's going to adopt me and sivilize me, and I can't stand it. I been there before.

Mr. Eliot properly praises this as "the only possible concluding sentence." But one sentence can hardly be advanced, as Mr. Eliot advances this one, to support the rightness of ten chapters. Moreover, if this sentence is right, then the rest of the conclusion is wrong, for its mean-

---

6 Gladys Bellamy (*Mark Twain as a Literary Artist,* Norman, Oklahoma, 1950, p. 221) has noted the insubstantial, dream-like quality of the image of the raft. Clemens thus discusses travel by raft in *A Tramp Abroad:* "The motion of the raft is . . . gentle, and gliding, and smooth, and noiseless; it calms down all feverish activities, it soothes to sleep all nervous . . . impatience; under its restful influence all the troubles and vexations and sorrows that harass the mind vanish away, and existence becomes a dream . . . a deep and tranquil ecstasy."

ing clashes with that of the final burlesque. Huck's decision to go west ahead of the inescapable advance of civilization is a confession of defeat. It means that the raft is to be abandoned. On the other hand, the jubilation of the family reunion and the proclaiming of Jim's freedom create a quite different mood. The tone, except for these last words, is one of unclouded success. I believe this is the source of the almost universal dissatisfaction with the conclusion. One can hardly forget that a bloody civil war did not resolve the issue.

Should Clemens have made Huck a tragic hero? Both Mr. Eliot and Mr. Trilling argue that that would have been a mistake, and they are very probably correct. But between the ending as we have it and tragedy in the fullest sense, there was vast room for invention. Clemens might have contrived an action which left Jim's fate as much in doubt as Huck's. Such an ending would have allowed us to assume that the principals were defeated but alive, and the quest unsuccessful but not abandoned. This, after all, would have been consonant with the symbols, the characters, and the theme as Clemens had created them—and with history.

Clemens did not acknowledge the truth his novel contained. He had taken hold of a situation in which a partial defeat was inevitable, but he was unable to—or unaware of the need to—give imaginative substance to that fact. If an illusion of success was indispensable, where was it to come from? Obviously Huck and Jim could not succeed by their own efforts. At this point Clemens, having only half escaped the genteel tradition, one of whose pre-eminent characteristics was an optimism undaunted by disheartening truth, returned to it. *Why* he did so is another story, having to do with his parents and his boyhood, with his own personality and his wife's, and especially with the character of his audience. But whatever the explanation, the faint-hearted ending of *The Adventures of Huckleberry Finn* remains an important datum in the record of American thought and imagination. It has been noted before, both by critics and non-professional readers. It should not be forgotten now.

To minimize the seriousness of what must be accounted a major flaw in so great a work is, in a sense, to repeat Clemens' failure of nerve. This is a disservice to criticism. Today we particularly need a criticism alert to lapses of moral vision. A measured appraisal of the failures and successes of our writers, past and present, can show us a great deal about literature and about ourselves. That is the critic's function. But he cannot perform that function if he substitutes considerations of technique for considerations of truth. Not only will such methods lead to errors of literary judgment, but beyond that, they may well encourage comparable evasions in other areas. It seems not unlikely, for instance, that the current preoccupation with matters of form is bound up with a tendency, by no means confined to literary quarters, to shy away from painful answers to complex questions of political morality. The conclusion to *The Adventures of Huckleberry Finn* shielded both Clemens and his audience from such an answer. But we ought not to be as tender-minded. For Huck Finn's besetting problem, the disparity between his best impulses and the behavior the community attempted to impose upon him, is as surely ours as it was Twain's.

The Unity and Coherence of *Huckleberry Finn*

by Richard P. Adams

The most obvious element of structure in *Huck Finn,* and the one most often noticed, is the picaresque journey down the river, full of inconsequently interspersed and apparently aimless adventures. But it is dangerous to say that much and stop, for the inconsequence does not preclude a plan, and the aimlessness is only apparent. Trilling, in discussing the special qualities of the river as a road, points out some profitable directions for further inquiry. The important thing, he says, is that the river is a moving road,

> . . . and the movement of the road in its own mysterious life transmutes the primitive simplicity of the form: the road itself is the greatest character in this novel of the road, and the hero's departures from the river and his returns to it compose a subtle and significant pattern. The linear simplicity of the picaresque novel is further modified by the story's having a clear dramatic organization: it has a beginning, a middle, and an end, and a mounting suspense of interest.[1]

Trilling perhaps oversimplifies the linear quality of the picaresque novel as Clemens knew it, but he does not overestimate the complexity of *Huck Finn,* and his observations on the "living" quality of the river and on the alternation of Huck's river and shore experiences are valuable clues.

Another clue, of perhaps even greater value, is furnished by James M. Cox's discussion of Huck's "initiation." According to Cox, the "fake murder" that Huck stages in order to get away from his father "is probably the most vital and crucial incident of the entire novel," [2] and Cox's observations on this event come close to defining the basic structure of the novel. The basic structure, which expresses the theme

"The Unity and Coherence of Huckleberry Finn*" by Richard P. Adams. From* Tulane Studies in English, *VI (1956), 89-103. Reprinted by permission of the author.*

1 Lionel Trilling, Introduction to the Rinehart edition of *The Adventures of Huckleberry Finn,* reprinted in *The Liberal Imagination* (New York, 1950), p. 115.
2 James M. Cox, "Remarks on the Sad Initiation of Huckleberry Finn," *Sewanee Review,* LXII (1954), 395.

of the boy's growth and which carries the weight of the incidents and the imagery throughout, is a pattern of symbolic death and rebirth. As Cox points out, the central action on the river begins with Huck's pretended death. It ends with his mistaken recognition as Tom by Aunt Sally Phelps, when he feels that "it was like being born again, I was so glad to find out who I was." This pattern is kept in the focus of the reader's attention, as Cox also observes, by repeated deaths and escapes occurring between, before, and after the main events.

The pattern of death and rebirth is reinforced by the pattern Trilling observes in Huck's departures from and returns to the river; only we need to reverse Trilling's terms, for it is Huck's departures from and returns to shore which are cognate and parallel to the pattern of death and rebirth. The same pattern provides the framework for the "clear dramatic organization" which Trilling notices, and it roughly determines the kind of beginning, middle, and end that the story has. Putting Cox and Trilling together, and oversimplifying for the sake of initial clarity, we can state a more nearly complete definition of the structure of *Huckleberry Finn*. The beginning is Huck's life on shore in and around the village of St. Petersburg with the Widow Douglas and Pap. The middle, initiated by Huck's fake death, is his withdrawal from the life of society and civilization to the river; this withdrawal is repeated after each of his adventures on land. The end is his equivocal rebirth, his qualified return, under a false identity and with many reservations, to civilized life at the Phelps plantation.

The pattern of death and rebirth is also intimately concerned in the "mounting suspense of interest" which Trilling notes. The theme of the book, as we have hinted, is the same as that of *Tom Sawyer:* the growth of a boy to manhood, and his final acceptance of adult moral responsibilities. In this connection the pattern of death and rebirth is more than a technical device. In the tradition of romantic literature, to which *Huck Finn* belongs, it is a form with a meaning. The growth of a boy to manhood is perhaps the most popular of all themes for romantic fiction, and the structure which best expresses it is that of the death-and-rebirth pattern. The reason for this association is based in romantic philosophy, according to which the individual human personality is conceived as an organism, which cannot undergo a fundamental change of any kind without being totally reconstituted. Its old self "dies" and its new self, an unpredictably different organism, is "born." Huck's initiation, his transformation from boy to man, is such a change. It is a radical reconstitution of his moral attitude toward the society in which he lives. He grows, therefore, during the time of crucial change, by "dying" out of society, withdrawing into nature on the river, and then returning or being "reborn" into society with a new and different attitude toward it.

It should not have to be said that this return is by no means an uncritical acceptance of conventional social values. The process of Huck's moral growth is, in fact, most emphatically indicated by his decision, made on three separate but closely related occasions, to free Jim from slavery, which is an act of rebellion against society. In a superficial sense the three decisions are the same, but each means more than the one before, because Huck knows more about the society he is deciding to oppose and because he sees more fully and clearly the implications of the decision and its probable consequences.

The context, which becomes increasingly solid and massive as Huck's knowledge increases, is a complex interrelationship of social, cultural, political, and economic forces. We might skeletonize it by making three simple statements, which we can then elaborate. First, slavery is evil. Second, the pseudo-aristocratic society of the ante-bellum South which fosters and depends on slavery is also evil. Third, the sentimental cultural veneer with which that society conceals its evil from itself, if not from others, is evil as well. These propositions apply with increasing cogency to Huck's three decisions, as he learns more about the character and workings, the concrete personal meanings and moral values, of Southern slave-holding aristocracy. The relations among these three intertwined thematic strands in *Huck Finn* are so complex and pervasive that a thorough explication of them would be longer than the book. I shall not try to exhaust them here, but rather to indicate their general character and, by exploring a few of them in some detail, to show how they work.

Huck's first decision to help Jim escape is made casually enough in the process of his own flight from civilization and from the domination of his father. When he comes across his fellow runaway on Jackson's Island, he is so glad to have his lonesomeness relieved by any sort of company that he hardly thinks of difficulties. " 'People would call me a low-down Abolitionist and despise me for keeping mum,' " he admits to Jim, " '—but that don't make no difference. I ain't a-going to tell, and I ain't a-going back there, anyways.' " But even this first and easiest decision is preceded by a fairly substantial development of motives and of symbolic motifs. Huck has been introduced to respectable society at the Widow's, where gentility is manifested painfully to him in regular hours, formal meals, and stiff clothing. When Miss Watson tells him about the bad place, he says he wishes he were there. "She got mad then, but I didn't mean no harm. All I wanted was to go somewheres. . . ." Later the same night, in harmony with the fake murder which is to come, he says, "I felt so lonesome I most wished I was dead." Then, in the planning and organization of Tom Sawyer's gang, we see Huck's indirect exposure to the culture of popular books and the sentimental proprieties of "high-toned" robbery and exploitation. Tom and the gang, of course, are completely unrealistic about the crimes they propose to commit, and blissfully unaware that crime, as gilded by the popular romances, is morally wrong. Farther on, Huck is regaled with Pap's reverse snobbishness on the subject of education and with his poor-white's groundless assertion of superiority over the much better educated "free nigger."

These lights and others like them are placed so as to reveal what Clemens considered to be the characteristic weaknesses, follies, and injustices of prewar Southern society. The essentially false and hypocritical gentility of the would-be aristocracy, the febrile and morally confusing sentimentalism of its favorite literature, and the crime of slavery which was the real basis of its economic and social system are continually brought home to Huck and the reader, in all kinds of dramatic, representative, and symbolic ways. The incidents are not haphazardly chosen or arranged. Each has its revealing gleam to contribute to Huck's unconsciously dawning awareness of the true values of the civilization to which he is being asked to belong. The result is that he runs away and, without any great misgivings at first, agrees to help Jim do the same.

The second decision is made necessary by a qualm of conscience. The fugitives are approaching Cairo, or think they are, and they both believe that Jim is almost free. Says Huck, "It hadn't ever come home to me before, what this thing was that I was doing. But now it did; and it stayed with me, and scorched me more and more." The point of difficulty is that freeing Jim involves robbing his owner, Miss Watson, of the eight hundred dollars he is worth on the market; and Jim makes the difficulty greater by threatening to have his children stolen, if necessary, by an Abolitionist. Huck is immediately and properly horrified. "It most froze me to hear such talk. . . . Here was this nigger, which I had as good as helped to run away, coming right out flat-footed and saying he would steal his children—children that belonged to a man I didn't even know; a man that hadn't ever done me no harm." The juxtaposition of "his" and "belonged" in this sentence, so carefully calculated to drive home the shocking injustice of property rights in human flesh, should not obscure the fact that there is a real moral issue. The great wrong of slavery does not make the lesser wrong of robbery right; a point which most pre-Civil War antislavery propagandists preferred to overlook. The issue is resolved by the fact that Huck finds himself unable to turn Jim in, for reasons which he does not fully understand but which the reader can surmise. To put it most simply, his human feelings are stronger than the commercial morality with which they are in conflict—as of course they should be. Unable to do entirely right, he chooses the lesser evil and goes on helping Jim.

When he repudiates his own conscience in this way, Huck takes a long step farther in his repudiation of Southern society, which has formed his conscience. He says to himself, in his usual innocent way, "what's the use you learning to do right when it's troublesome to do right and ain't no trouble to do wrong, and the wages is just the same? . . . So I reckoned I wouldn't bother no more about it, but after this always do whichever come handiest at the time." The innocence is of Huck, not Clemens, and it represents a remarkably keen penetration into the difficult question of personal or individual morality in relation to social conventions. Huck realizes in practice, though never in conscious theory, that the question is not one of a simple conflict between the individual and the mass, or the social institution, but that the two interpenetrate, and that the individual conscience is usually an ally of the social pressure for conformity.

Thoreau, in "Civil Disobedience," feels himself on solid ground when his conscience tells him to oppose the extension of slavery and the government that sanctions and promotes it. "If," he says, "the injustice . . . is of such a nature that it requires you to be the agent of injustice to another, then, I say, break the law." That seems comparatively easy; all that is needed is the courage to stand up against the government, which Southerners have always had in abundance. But, when the ante-bellum conscience is formed in Missouri instead of Massachusetts, the battle becomes intensely complicated. Its lines are drawn mostly inside the personality, which is then divided against itself. As Trilling remarks, it is the paradox in Huck's own thinking, by the terms of which he does right by doing what he thoroughly believes, in his conscious mind, to be wrong, that makes his character heroic and Clemens's satire brilliant.[3] His battle is desperate, his victory sublime. If it is fine to follow as Thoreau does the dictates of conscience over law, it is finer and much more difficult to follow those of the right over conscience and law combined.

*   *   *

The third and final decision is led up to by a more personal and extensive experience of upperclass Southerners than before. Shortly after the second crisis, Huck and Jim realize that they have passed Cairo in the fog, but before they can do anything to get back, the raft is wrecked by a steamboat and they are separated again. Huck finds himself ashore, beginning a new phase of the story and of his education. His shore adventures alternate, from this point on, with repeated escapes to the river, until he comes to the Phelps plantation. These adventures bring him more dramatically than before into contact, and

8 Trilling, pp. 111-12.

more often into conflict, with aristocrats of various kinds. The increase of experience, knowledge, and understanding which he gains in this phase leads convincingly to his ultimate decision to repudiate aristocratic society by freeing its victim Jim.

The first aristocrats he meets in person, leaving aside the Widow, Miss Watson, and Judge Thatcher, are the Grangerfords, by whom he is strongly impressed and who are genuinely impressive in many ways. They have the typical aristocratic virtues: they are dignified, hospitable, proud, handsome, cultured (after a fashion), courteous, devout, and kind to strangers and dependents. But the more Huck learns of them, the more uneasy he becomes about their character and behavior. Clemens, through Huck's observations and comments, gradually undercuts the value of their culture. The description of the house, which is parallel to the account of "The House Beautiful" in *Life on the Mississippi*, is a skillful piece of irony. Huck admires the place immensely, while Clemens mercilessly exposes the queer mixture of arrogant show and pathetic provincialism that it presents to even a moderately sophisticated eye. The description leads up to and is ludicrously topped off by Huck's account of Emmeline Grangerford's esthetic misdeeds in crayon and verse, of the graveyard school run wild and gone to seed. The cultural pretensions of the aristocracy are, by this report, sufficiently harmless in themselves but crude, anachronistic, and highly absurd from any civilized modern point of view.

The feud which is going on between the Grangerfords and the Shepherdsons is a much more serious matter, and it does not depend on the same kind of irony for its effect. It is as deeply horrifying to Huck as it could possibly be to Clemens. The brutal killing of the two boys makes Huck so sick that he cannot even tell about it in detail without getting sick again; and his admiration for the better qualities of the aristocrats is more than canceled by this result of their violence.

The incident is a direct expression of feeling on the part of its author. In *Life on the Mississippi* Clemens goes somewhat out of his way to comment on a published opinion that the South had "the highest type of civilization this continent has seen . . ." He demonstrates the hollowness of the brag in a footnote with "Illustrations of it thoughtlessly omitted by the advertiser," consisting of newspaper accounts of four fights in which five Southern gentlemen were killed and one injured, with the usual incidental damage to bystanders, reference also being made to four other murders and one nonfatal stabbing in previous engagements involving some of the same gentlemen. The people concerned were of the highest class that Southern civilization had produced, including a general and his son, a bank president, a college professor, and "two 'highly connected' young Virginians" who fought a duel with butcher knives. It is from this kind of violence that Huck escapes to the river again, wishing that he "hadn't ever come ashore that night to see such things. I ain't ever going to get shut of them—lots of times I dream about them." Clemens had often dreamed about some violent episodes he witnessed as a boy.

Huck's reaction leads to one of his most lyric descriptions of the freedom, comfort, and beauty of the river, and the loveliness of life on a raft. But evil comes into this world also, in the shape of the two confidence men who palm themselves off as "the rightful Duke of Bridgewater" and "the late Dauphin . . . Looy the Seventeen, son of Looy the Sixteen and Marry Antonette," and who take over in the true aristocratic, robber-gang fashion. The cream of the jest is that the duke's claim is accepted by the other rogue so that he may in turn make his higher claim. The cream of the cream is that the duke then has to admit the king's superior status and rights in order that both may exploit the plebeian members of the little commonwealth. But the richest layer of all is Huck's good-naturedly cynical accommodation to the whole arrangement. He sees immediately what frauds these are, but he is pleased when the duke knuckles under; "for what you want, above all things, on a raft, is for everybody to be satisfied, and feel right and kind towards the others."

Clemens's feeling about the kind of imposition practiced—or at least attempted—here is given in [a] notebook entry: "There are shams and shams; there are frauds and frauds, but the transparentest of all is the sceptered one. We see monarchs meet and go through solemn ceremonies, farces, with straight countenances; but it is not possible to imagine them meeting in private and not laughing in each other's faces." [4] The fraud practiced by the bogus king and duke is no different from the frauds put over by real kings and dukes, except that the latter are bigger. As Huck explains to Jim, after the confidence men have worked over their first town together, they are lucky not to have Henry VIII on their hands, for he was a really accomplished crook; " 'If we'd 'a' had him along 'stead of our kings he'd 'a' fooled that town a heap worse than ourn done. I don't say that ourn is lambs, because they ain't, when you come right down to the cold facts; but they ain't nothing to *that* old ram, anyway.' " This observation reinforces the point already made, implicitly, that the Grangerfords and Shepherdsons, by their more serious imitation of aristocratic ways, are only presenting a more pernicious version of something which at best is a sham and a fraud.

Perhaps the most emphatic impression of the ugly side of Southern chivalry is given by the incident in which Huck witnesses the cold-

4 *Mark Twain's Notebook,* ed. A. B. Paine (New York and London, 1935), p. 196. Clemens neglected this view when he later met some royal persons himself.

blooded murder of old Boggs by Colonel Sherburn. Boggs is a noisy but harmless fool, Sherburn a fine example of aristocratic pride—brave and intelligent in his own way, but narrow, selfish, inconsiderate, harsh, and brutal. It is, again, a sickening scene, and it is based on a murder that Clemens witnessed as a boy. But it may be that the importance of the incident for the satirical aspect of the book lies mainly in the character of the townspeople, who are by and large a degraded lot. "There couldn't anything wake them up all over," says Huck, "and make them happy all over, like a dog-fight—unless it might be putting turpentine on a stray dog and setting fire to him, or tying a tin pan to his tail and see him run himself to death." They try half-heartedly to get Boggs to stop his offensive yelling and go home, but they also perversely enjoy the shooting and the old man's death, the view of the body in the drug store window, and the reenactment of the murder by one of the onlookers. When they go to Sherburn's house with the announced intention of lynching him, he lectures them contemptuously and drives them off with a shotgun, which he does not have to fire.

His contempt seems justified, on the face of things. These are the same people who, after hooting the Shakespearean efforts of the king and duke, prove ripe for the Royal Nonesuch hoax. The duke, in his estimate of them, agrees with Sherburn. He prints at the foot of his handbill "LADIES AND CHILDREN NOT ADMITTED," remarking, " 'There . . . if that line don't fetch them, I don't know Arkansaw!' " It does. But the deeper point is not explicitly stated here, or anywhere else in *Huck Finn*, nor is it fully understood, we may suppose, by either Sherburn or the duke. They see well enough that the people are ignorant, cowardly, and gullible; they do not see that the reason for that fact is the apparently opposite fact that an aristocracy is in power. Clemens, however, was aware of it and well convinced that poverty, both of the flesh and of the spirit, is the mirror image of aristocratic splendor and that universal cruelty is inevitably characteristic of any society divided into rigid classes with hereditary inequalities of function, privilege, and status.

This principle is explained more clearly in *A Connecticut Yankee.* The Yankee is shocked at the way poor peasants in Arthurian England rush out, heedless of right or justice, and help each other hang their neighbors in their lord's behalf, apparently unable "to see anything horrible about it." His comment is almost a direct reference to the satire in *Huck Finn.*

> It reminded me of a time thirteen centuries away, when the "poor whites" of our South who were always despised and frequently insulted by the slave-lords around them, and who owed their base condition simply to the presence of slavery in their midst, were yet pusillanimously ready

to side with the slave-lords in all political moves for the upholding and perpetuating of slavery, and did also finally shoulder their muskets and pour out their lives in an effort to prevent the destruction of that very institution which degraded them. And there was only one redeeming feature connected with that pitiful piece of history; and that was, that secretly the "poor white" did detest the slave-lord, and did feel his own shame.

The Yankee also remarks that "It is enough to make a body ashamed of his race to think of the sort of froth that has always occupied its thrones without shadow of right or reason," and what Clemens obviously means is that any respectable race would blow such froth to the moon before letting it settle into power.

Huck, whose background is about as purely poor-white as it could be, is given almost exactly the same words—"It was enough to make a body ashamed of the human race"—to describe his feelings about the next incident. The king and duke are having a fine run of initial success in playing their confidence game on the Wilks girls and most of their neighbors. It is a game that Huck perfectly understands, and he becomes so much ashamed of himself for being involved in it, though unwillingly, that he takes the risky measure of telling the truth in order to break it up. The most painful aspect of the affair applies directly to the theme of slavery, being the inhumanity of the fake aristocrats in the sale of the Wilks family slaves, "the two sons up the river to Memphis, and their mother down the river to Orleans." Huck says again that "it most made me down sick to see it. . . . I can't ever get it out of my memory, the sight of them poor miserable girls and niggers hanging around each other's necks and crying . . ." The reader is likely to recall, as Clemens must have done, that this is not something only fakers do; it is precisely what Miss Watson does in planning to sell Jim "down to Orleans"; the general truth is that, as the Connecticut Yankee remarks in another place, "a privileged class, an aristocracy, is but a band of slaveholders under another name." The function of the king and duke is to show this basic identity, and underscore its meaning. Are these two scoundrels the most absurd, unmitigated, bare-faced buffoons of wickedness imaginable? So, Clemens wishes us to feel and understand, are all aristocrats. Kings, dukes, pirates, robbers, confidence men, and slaveholders are the same, and all sorry. Anyone who respects them is a fool, anyone who fears them is a coward, and anyone who supports them or submits to them is a slave himself.

Huck is none of these things, though he is almost infinitely good-natured and accommodating. He goes along with the king and duke as well and as long as he can, and he feels sorry for them when the mob escorts them out of town, in tar and feathers, on a rail. But he spoils their game with the Wilkses, and he leaves them when the king sells Jim into bondage again. For him, their function has been to complete his education in the social realities of slavocracy and to put the finishing touches on his preparation for the final decision he has to make. They have done the job effectively; he is ready now to see Jim through to freedom in spite of anything. Unconsciously, but with deep conviction, he understands the society to which by accident of birth he belongs, and refuses to submit to it.

On this last occasion, Huck sees his problem as being more difficult than it has ever seemed to him before, because it presents itself to him in terms of the religious sanction which the institution of slavery enjoyed in the prewar South. His conscience, unable to win the battle alone, now tells him, in accordance with the Sunday-school teaching he feels he should have had, " 'that people that acts as I'd been acting about that nigger goes to everlasting fire.' " Again, Huck is expressing one of his author's ideas. Clemens remarks of his mother in the *Autobiography* that,

> kind-hearted and compassionate as she was, I think she was not conscious
> that slavery was a bald, grotesque, and unwarrantable usurpation. She had
> never heard it assailed in any pulpit, but had heard it defended and
> sanctified in a thousand; her ears were familiar with Bible texts that ap-
> proved it, but if there were any that disapproved it they had not been
> quoted by her pastors; as far as her experience went, the wise and the
> good and the holy were unanimous in the conviction that slavery was
> right, righteous, sacred, the peculiar pet of the Deity, and a condition
> which the slave himself ought to be daily and nightly thankful for.[5]

Huck has easily won out over public opinion, less easily over public opinion reinforced by his own conscience. The addition of the Deity to the list of powers with which he has to contend raises his battle to its ultimate pitch of intensity.

His first maneuver is to pray for the improvement of his character, but he realizes at once that the plea is hypocritical. To make it good, he writes a letter to Miss Watson to tell her where Jim is, but he gets to thinking about Jim's goodness and loyalty and kindness, and all the times they have helped each other, and again he makes up his mind.

> I was a-trembling, because I'd got to decide, forever, betwixt two things,
> and I knowed it. I studied a minute, sort of holding my breath, and then
> says to myself:
> "All right, then, I'll *go* to hell"—and tore it up.
> It was awful thoughts and awful words, but they was said. And I let
> them stay said; and never thought no more about reforming.

[5] *Mark Twain's Autobiography*, ed. A. B. Paine (New York and London, 1924), I, 123.

With this decision, the middle or river section comes to its conclusion, and the ending of the book begins.

Clemens obviously had difficulty handling the ending. The reason seems to be that once Huck's final decision is made there is no longer any important part for Jim to play. His function in relation to the theme has been to test, or to furnish occasions when events would test, Huck's growing moral strength and mature independence. When that has been done, to the last possible extreme, Jim needs simply to be got out of the book as quickly and as unobtrusively as possible. Instead, Clemens plays up Tom Sawyer's long, elaborate, and almost meaningless escape plot. The final solution to the problem, the disclosure that Miss Watson has died and freed Jim in her will, is all that is needed, and the less said about it the better. And yet the escape plot is not altogether irrelevant. It furthers and completes the satire on sentimental literature, from which Tom draws his inspirations. It caps the ridicule of aristocratic pretensions by identifying Jim, the imprisoned slave, with the noble persons on whose renowned adventures his liberation is modeled. It is an immense expression of contempt for adult society, so easily and so thoroughly hoodwinked by a pair of audacious children; and the more absurd Tom's antics become, the more the satire is built up. It is as much an attack on conventional respectability as Huck's discomforts at the Widow Douglas's, or his observations on the culture of the Grangerfords, or his rebellion against slavery itself.

Huck's attitude at the end is a mixture, full of ironies and reservations of many kinds. Having made the great decision to repudiate society, physically, morally, and spiritually, he can hardly return to it without equivocation. In a sense, his acceptance of the name and status of Tom Sawyer on the Phelps plantation is a return, but it is made on completely false premises. Also Huck is glad in a way to submit to Tom's leadership and direction. The burden of lonely responsibility has weighed long and heavily. But he is not fooled for a minute into thinking that there is any validity in Tom's adherence to bookish or aristocratic authority. " 'When I start in to steal a nigger,' " he says, " 'I ain't no ways particular how it's done so it's done. What I want is my nigger . . . and I don't give a dead rat what the authorities thinks about it nuther.' " He has arrived at maturity and self-sufficiency, and he is poised at the end in a delicate balance, ready at any moment "to light out for the territory" in order to escape Aunt Sally's threatened continuation of the civilizing process begun by the Widow Douglas.

This aspect of the conclusion is exactly right. It would have been wrong—impossible in fact—for Clemens to bring the story to a stop, as he might have tried to do by having Huck accept the moral values of society and return to it uncritically in a "happy ending." The whole process of his development runs counter to any such result. The impression that Clemens has to leave, and does leave, in the reader's mind and feelings is that Huck will continue to develop. He will escape again, as many times as he needs to, from society and any of its restrictions which would hamper or prevent his growth. He will die and be reborn whenever his character needs to break the mold that society would place upon it. Accordingly, the structure of the story is left open; the conclusion is deliberately inconclusive.

Frank Baldanza, who has made the most direct attack so far on the problem of structure in *Huck Finn,* believes that the basic principle can be defined as rhythmic repetition, with variation and development, of many thematic motifs, which have the effect of stitching the book together internally. He further suggests that each recurrence "was impulsive on Twain's part, and that any pattern we find in the repetitions is either unconsciously or accidentally ordained." [6] My analysis would seem to bear out the observation that rhythmic, varied, and developmental repetition is important. It is not basic to the structure, but it certainly does support it and supply it with a texture of rich and complex harmony. However, this effect is not and cannot possibly be accidental; it fits too well with the larger thematic repetition of Huck's decision. And I suspect very strongly too that Clemens must have been aware of it, in some way, as being appropriate to the pattern of the work he meant to make. A close examination will show that the motifs most often repeated are those most intimately concerned with the aristocracy-slavery-sentimentalism relationship. Moreover the variations add up to a steady intensification of Huck's and the reader's awareness of the injustice, the hypocrisy, and the general moral ugliness and weakness of Southern society before the war. This intensification provides the milieu and the measure of Huck's development through the death-and-rebirth pattern from irresponsible boyhood to moral maturity.

The total result of these thematic, structural, and symbolic workings is a novel which has a remarkably high degree of consistency, coherence, and unity. Its theme is the growth of an individual personality. Its crisis is the moral decision, repeated three times, to repudiate the conventions of society and do the individually, humanly right thing. Its rising interest is given by the sharply increasing complexity of the individual awareness of the implications of such an action. Its structure is defined by the extinction of the old childish organization of mind and feelings, the symbolic death of the individual as he was, his withdrawal from society into nature, and his reconstitution, or sym-

<hr>

[6] Frank Baldanza, "The Structure of *Huckleberry Finn,*" *American Literature,* XXVII (November, 1955), 353.

bolic rebirth, on a higher and more mature level of organization, as a better, more capable person. The theme and structure are concretely embodied and related in the texture, which reinforces both with a rhythmically repeated and varied pattern of appropriate motifs and images. The functional, organic interrelations of all these factors must have something to do with the effect of unity which readers generally feel in *Huckleberry Finn,* but which we are now only beginning to understand and be able to explain.

The Moral Structure of *Huckleberry Finn*

by Gilbert M. Rubenstein

The greatness of *Huckleberry Finn* has always seemed so self-evident that we are distinctly surprised to find it obscured or actually denied by two articles in a recent number (October, 1955) of *College English*.[1] But perhaps it is a good thing to have our most cherished convictions examined, if only that we may more firmly realize the ground on which we stand. Beginning with an analysis of each of the aforementioned articles, the present paper will attempt to show how a more constructive evaluation may be achieved by concentrating attention upon the undeniable moral structure of the book. It is my contention that *Huckleberry Finn* should be approached simply, directly, *realistically*—precisely as Mark Twain wrote it.

I

The first article, by Mr. Lauriat Lane, Jr., does indeed pay a passing tribute to the moral realism of the book, but then "extends" it into fantastic patterns of allegory and symbolism. For example, the river journey becomes something out of Rimbaud. Huck is described as "drifting" and "passive"; the "nakedness" of the two friends becomes a symbol of their shucking off "the excrescences of the real world" and their coming "as close as possible to the world of the spirit." Now the actual facts are plain. The very last word one should use to describe Huck is "passive." He is no drifter but a plucky, lovable boy who, after painful self-examination, achieves an iron determination to help his friend Jim reach free territory. Their journey together *has* a destination, and it is not, as Lane suggests, an "escape" from "the real world"; it is rather an escape from slavery into freedom, *within* a real world which amply contains both conditions of mankind. They are bound

"The Moral Structure of Huckleberry Finn" *by Gilbert M. Rubenstein. From* College English, *XVIII (November, 1956), 72-76. Reprinted by permission of the author and the National Council of Teachers of English.*
[1] Lauriat Lane, Jr., "Why *Huckleberry Finn* Is a Great World Novel," XVII, 1-5; William Van O'Connor, "Why *Huckleberry Finn* Is Not the Great American Novel," XVII, 6-10. [ED.]

for Cairo, Illinois, there to find passage for Jim up the Ohio River into a free land. And if they occasionally relax and enjoy the trip by swimming, loafing, or fishing, what harm is done? Their major goal is never forgotten—as witness Jim's eager expectation of reaching Cairo and his bitter, fearful disappointment at having overshot it during the fog. The river is not an end but a means to an end. It has no "basic symbolic pattern" beyond the general connotation of freedom. Nor are Huck and Jim noticeably more naked on the raft than they are ashore, except when swimming, possibly! Mr. Lane has evidently been influenced by Eliot's "strong brown god" interpretation of the river (repeated with variations by Trilling in his famous and otherwise excellent essay on the novel). But the symbolic interpretation is quite misleading and unnecessary, to say the least. Huck Finn, though no churchgoer, is *not* a pagan; and the moral structure of the book is deeply moving, in the best Judaeo-Christian tradition.

The article winds up with some ultra-profound observations about Huck's "symbolic death" and assumption of various identities, "as far removed from . . . reality as possible." Once again a simpler, more realistic interpretation would be preferable. There are sound reasons in the plot for Huck to pretend to be dead (he must escape the ever-present threat of his father) and to assume the disguises he takes (he must shield Jim and himself and obtain information to facilitate their mutual escape). His lies and evasions, as Trilling correctly recognizes, are the boy's only weapons against physically stronger adult foes. Huck's courage and dedication are truly inspiring. It is a pity, then, that Mr. Lane chose to defend the book by "extending" it into a symbolic pattern that it simply does not possess. At other points in the article, however, he makes some more meaningful attempts at extension—though these are never adequately explored. For instance, Lane speaks of the book as being related to *Don Quixote* in its theme of "appearance versus reality"; but he fails to relate the character of Huck and Jim to the realistic Sancho Panza or Tom Sawyer to the romantic knight. Lane makes still another comparison in a very brief paragraph linking the book to other novels of education (*Candide, Tom Jones,* and *Ulysses*), in which the hero "goes forth into life that he may learn." But *what* Huck learns Lane never makes clear.

II

If Mr. Lane's analysis of the novel goes astray because of unrewarding "extensions" of reality into allegory and symbolism, the second article, by William Van O'Connor, commits the graver fault of misreading the realities of the book entirely. In a harsh attack on *Huckleberry Finn,* O'Connor finds it not to be a work of art because of serious "flaws," primarily an "imperfect sense of tone." First he criticizes Jim

for using the raft to escape downstream and asks why Jim didn't simply "strike out for the Illinois shore and freedom." But these objections
are answered very clearly in Ch. 8 (p. 44, Rinehart ed.), where Jim
tells of his original plans for escape: he was afraid to flee on foot for
fear of being tracked by dogs, and it would have been unwise to steal
a skiff to cross over the river because the skiff would have been missed
and traced to a likely position on the Illinois shore. He intended to
slip ashore some twenty-five miles downstream, by taking hold of a
passing raft, but was prevented—luckily for him, as Huck later discovers (in Ch. 11), for Jim would surely have been captured by eager
people on the Illinois shore who were on the lookout for a runaway
Negro "murderer" of Huck Finn. The only possible goal then was
Cairo, far downstream.

The second example of "imperfect tone" involves what O'Connor
calls Tom's "highjinks" at the end of the book which are "anti-climac-
tic" because Miss Watson's will has already freed Jim. Properly understood, however, the ending is but the final example of one of the main
themes—the contrast between realism and romance (to be explained
further below); it is in perfect keeping with Tom's imaginative nature (see Chs. 2 and 3) and ends the book on a stimulating note of
dramatic irony. O'Connor finds additional evidence of what he calls
"melodrama" in Huck's relationship with his father, in the shooting
of Boggs, and in the tarring and feathering of the Duke and Dauphin;
but he does not explain *why* any of these examples is melodramatic.
Thousands of upright boys have had the misfortune of a bullying,
worthless father. The Boggs episode gives Twain a splendid chance
to expose mass cowardice in addition to the cowardice of Boggs himself; perhaps Boggs did not deserve his end, but nobody can say he
didn't ask for it. As to the tarring and feathering of the Duke and
Dauphin, it seems perfectly clear that sooner or later their confidence
game would backfire, and their particular kind of punishment was
usual then on the frontier—not only usual but eminently just. They
have assumed different aliases and costumes throughout the book: let
them get out of *that* costume!

It would be wearisome to refute the few additional examples that
O'Connor gives of "imperfect tone," but one major charge must still
be answered. This is the very specious claim that Twain once lost
sight of Huck's moral sensitivity towards Jim after they were separated
by the steamboat which smashed their raft and Huck was taken in by
the Grangerfords. Huck is condemned for not thinking of Jim during
his involvement "for many days, perhaps weeks" with the affairs of
the other people; and O'Connor does not find Huck sufficiently de-
monstrative when the servant Jack leads him to the overjoyed Jim. But
he has neglected to say that when they were separated Huck "sung
out for Jim about a dozen times" (p. 94); Huck may well have con-

cluded that Jim had been drowned. Anyhow, the moment he sets foot on shore he is stopped in his tracks by the Grangerfords' dogs, and events thereafter move so rapidly toward a climax that Huck, a virtual prisoner, has no opportunity to look for Jim even if he should think Jim to be alive. In the Grangerford-Shepherdson feud, incidentally, Huck shows plenty of his usual "moral sensitivity" to the tragic death of little Buck. O'Connor tries to give the impression that Twain has forgotten the Huck-Jim relationship too long, but in fact less than two chapters elapse before the two are reunited; and into those chapters Twain has packed a world of meaning relevant to his major theme (as I shall show below). Finally Huck is *not* cold to Jim when they meet. He is shocked, as well he might be! "I poked into the place a ways and . . . found a man laying there asleep—and, by jings, it was my old Jim!" After Jim's brief account of their separation he asks the natural question: "Why didn't you tell my Jack to fetch me here sooner, Jim?" Considering all these circumstances and also considering what we already know about Huck's attachment to Jim (remember the famous apology which Huck makes only a chapter before he is separated from Jim), is it fair to say, as O'Connor does, that Huck is "indifferent" to Jim's fate? O'Connor also finds fault with Jim, incidentally, for not replying to Huck's calls when they were separated in the river. "Presumably one reply would have quieted Huck and made detection much less likely." Would it have been heard against the "booming current" and the noisy steamboat that "started her engines ten seconds after she stopped them"? (p. 94) Additional calls would certainly have brought upon Jim the dogs which trapped Huck. Jim did not *know* that there were dogs there; but he was shrewd enough to expect dogs everywhere on shore and to fear them (see p. 111).

All these critical distortions—and more—about Mark Twain's masterpiece he has managed to cram into less than three pages of text, but these are "pie" to the irrelevancies that fill the remaining half of O'Connor's article in which he speaks about the author's life, about Abraham Lincoln, and other persons. There is, particularly, a long discussion of the uncivilized, passive hero in Hemingway's novels—like the "uncivilized" and "passive" Huck, presumably; in this digression O'Connor sneers at the "innocence" and "irresponsibility" of Hemingway's characters and those of Sherwood Anderson. He equates irresponsibility with a refusal to "make the [unspecified] compromises all civilized people make."

III

What then is *Huckleberry Finn* about? Nothing that the ordinary reader—not given to supersubtle speculations and distortions, but possessed only of common sense and a responsive heart—would fail to understand and appreciate. The clarity and directness of insight, the humorous but sharp exposure of human failings on the one hand and the warm faith in human goodness and equality on the other—these are the substance of the novel; these are the qualities that have endeared the book to common humanity all over the world and have indeed made it a "great world novel."

The major theme is stated succinctly at the end of Ch. 33 (p. 232), when Huck feels compassion even for the feathered frauds: "Human beings *can* be awful cruel to one another." This theme is central to every aspect of the plot and characterization. Human cruelty applies primarily, of course, to the life of the saintly but hunted Jim, whose history personifies all of the evils of slavery. Twain makes a sharp distinction between two types of cruelty—the deliberate callousness of the hard-hearted, and the unintentional or thoughtless indifference of the normally kind-hearted. Examples of the first type are Pap's cruelty toward Huck, or the Duke and Dauphin's cruelty toward Jim (the Dauphin actually sells Jim for forty dollars—forty pieces of silver) and toward the three Wilks girls they attempt to defraud. As examples of less deliberate cruelty there is Miss Watson's initial thoughtless desire to sell faithful Jim, the event which starts the entire plot; there is the senseless, ancient feud which ends the lives of so many good Grangerfords and Shepherdsons, including the pathetic thirteen-year-old Buck; there is the unthinking, automatic chaining of Jim by kindly Uncle Silas and Aunt Sally (he can preach lofty sermons, and she can weep for "Sid"). Most notably there is Huck's one fault, his earlier attitude of "superiority" to Jim, a feeling quite understandable in any Southern white boy of that day but one which—to his everlasting credit—he forces himself to reject. It should be added that his prejudice never does Jim any harm except for the one practical joke, which backfires on Huck and teaches him a permanent lesson.

This idea of the two types of cruelty relates Twain's world view to those other novelists of the realistic tradition that he resembles most closely—Fielding and Dickens. All three authors look at people in much the same way, dividing them into three classes. On the one hand, we have a few saintly characters, those who are almost always naturally good—like Huck, Jim, Widow Douglas, Aunt Sally, and the three sweet Wilks girls; examples in Fielding and Dickens include Parson Adams, Joseph Andrews, Fanny, Pickwick, Joe Gargery, and Biddy. On the other hand, there are also the two more faulty types mentioned above: numerous well-meaning but sometimes thoughtless ones, who in the English novelists include Squire Western, Tom Jones, David Copperfield, Pip, or Provis; and a few cold-blooded ones—for example, Lady Booby, Parson Trulliber, Bill Sykes, Estella, and Jaggers. The saintly persons, of course, require no major alteration of character; and the cold-blooded ones are usually beyond redemption, as the new judge, for example, can testify with his efforts to "reform" Pap. It is the large middle group, particularly, in all three novelists which can be redeemed out of their false pride or selfishness—these are usually the besetting sins. But their redemption, if it comes at all, comes only as a result of deep searching by the individual into his own heart; it does not come by merely paying lip service to the dogmas or rituals of organized religion. A good example of this fact may be found in Ch. 18 of *Huckleberry Finn,* in which Huck describes the Grangerfords and Shepherdsons going to church, carrying their guns along. "It was pretty ornery preaching—all about brotherly love, and suchlike tiresomeness; but everybody said it was a good sermon, and they all talked it over going home, and had such a powerful lot to say about good works and free grace and preforeordestination, and I don't know what all, that it did seem to me to be one of the roughest Sundays I had run across yet." The next day the feud is resumed, and Buck is shot down. Only the lovers get away from their murderous families. The false pride inherent in the whole unexamined, traditional code of "quality" is here clearly exposed, and so is the solution to the evils that false pride brings. The solution, simply, is human love, the generally unapplied lesson of the sermon—love between Sophia and Harney, between Huck and Jim, between black and white, between human beings everywhere.

Another important theme in the book, which runs parallel to the main idea already discussed and which frequently fuses with it, is the conflict between romance and realism. This opposition comes out clearly in the contrast between Huck and Tom. Tom is an imaginative boy, who must invest the most prosaic facts of life with a glamorous aura (a Sunday-school picnic becomes a "whole parcel of Spanish merchants and rich A-rabs") and who never does anything in a simple way when there is a more complicated method available which will appeal to his romantic fancy; Huck is just the reverse—to him a spade is always a spade. Of course Twain prefers Huck's mature, forthright directness to Tom's day-dreaming, which results in unintentional cruelty to Jim. This distinction between the two boys explains the nature of the overlong conclusion of the novel, but the distinction is applied to other persons and situations throughout the book, in perhaps more meaningful ways. The whole idea of monarchy, in the persons of the Duke and Dauphin and in the very funny and pertinent colloquy between Huck and Jim about King Solomon's wisdom, is satirized as a cruel romantic delusion; the colloquy is all the funnier because, for once, Huck himself has been trapped by the romantic lore he has picked up from Tom, as Jim realistically explodes Huck's "logic." Also the cruelty inherent in the concept of chivalry and aristocracy, as embodied by the Grangerfords and Shepherdsons, is exposed as being the inevitable result of the senseless romantic tradition of duelling and feuding. Most important of all, the notion of race superiority, the whole code of white supremacy, is revealed as romantic nonsense. We see this idea not only in the story of Huck and Jim but also in the foul anti-Negro rantings of Pap Finn, earlier in the book (Ch. 6), a superb example of Know-Nothingism. The spirit of democracy, according to Mark Twain, is not to be found in the romantic myths of class or racial superiority. Human beings are superior to one another only in the goodness of their hearts and in their love for other people.

This is not the place to enlarge upon the many other fine qualities of Twain's masterpiece—his wonderfully accurate ear for colloquial speech, the naturalness with which the story begins and ends, the photographic eye for realistic physical detail, the inclusion of national types, and so on. But meanwhile it can surely be said that the moral structure of the book alone teaches timeless lessons to all humanity.

"So Noble . . . and So Beautiful a Book"

by *Walter Blair*

It is so noble a book and so beautiful a book, that I don't want it to
have even trivial faults in it.
—S. L. Clemens' marginal comment in his copy of W. E. H.
Lecky, *History of European Morals*, II, 39.

In addition to portraying scenes, characters, and actions in a better
style and more richly, *Huckleberry Finn* surpassed *Tom Sawyer* in
commenting on what its author in time would call "the damned human race." Scenes in early chapters embody certain beliefs: the robber
gang scenes, a loathing of posturings in romantic fiction; and the account of the judge's attempt to reform Pap, a dislike of sentimentality.

These scenes are isolated; and so are others of 1876 which dramatize
ideas and attitudes. Twain had not found a comprehensive theme or
ways to develop it at length. Some of his reading and his ponderings
about that reading, though, eventually would help him discover a
significant theme; and he would learn how to make it permeate much
of the book. Some early passages predict these important developments, one stimulated by an old favorite, Carlyle, the rest by a newly
discovered author whose concepts would be very influential—W. E. H.
Lecky.

* * *

Several passages written in 1876 deal with problems of morality: in
these was the germ of the chief thought to be developed in the com-
pleted novel. Huck's attacks on prayer and his concepts of heaven in
chapters i-iii introduce this motif. One should picture Clemens reading these of an evening to the Quarry Farm household, his eyes glanc-
ing mischievously from beneath feathery eyebrows at Susan Crane. For
Mrs. Crane was a pious woman; frequently Clemens invaded her gar-

den to argue about her orthodox beliefs. The ironic nicknames which
the pair used were products of their controversies: he called her Sinful
Susan, and she called him Holy Samuel. The passages made fun of
some of these arguments.

Her husband Theodore also would have listened to these chapters
with interest, for they echo a book which he and Clemens had discovered two summers before and since then had read and discussed
while lolling in hammocks on the lawn.[1] It was a favorite of Clemens
for years: he called it "noble" and "beautiful," and plentiful under-
linings and marginal notations through both volumes attest to his
having read the surviving copy (and perhaps another copy which has
disappeared) carefully and thoughtfully.[2]

W. E. H. Lecky, an English-Scottish-Irish historian, had leaped to
fame at twenty-seven by publishing his *History of Rationalism* in 1865.
The book which Clemens and Crane were reading was Lecky's latest,
even more popular than his first, *History of European Morals from
Augustus to Charlemagne,* a ponderous two-volumer published in 1869.

Lecky's book is in some ways comparable with H. G. Wells' *Outline
of History* and the simplification of Arnold Toynbee's simplification
of history, best sellers in the twentieth century. Concentrating upon
uncomplicated lines of narrative and eschewing minutiae, it covers
great spans of time; it provides picturesque details; it is lucid in style.
So it was likely to appeal to amateur historians.

Also it dealt with problems about morality such as Clemens had
often discussed—favorite problems for theologians—the nature of morality, the extent of moral responsibility. Along the margins of Clemens' copy of Darwin's *The Descent of Man* (New York, 1871)—now
in the University of California Library—Clemens earlier had started a
discussion which he continued in Lecky's margins. When Darwin, in
his chapter on "Moral Sense," discussed theories about the origin of
morals, Clemens had made a comment (I, 78) indicating that he
thought moral decisions were motivated by "selfishness . . . not char-
ity nor generosity." Lecky, whom Darwin cites, is much concerned
with this problem.

---

1 *What Is Man?* (Definitive Edition), XXVI, ix.
2 Chester L. Davis, ed., "Mark Twain's Religious Beliefs as Indicated by Notations
in His Books," *The Twainian,* May-June, July-August, September-October, Novem-
ber-December, 1956, describes an 1874 edition inscribed "F. W. Crane 1874" and
"S. L. Clemens 1906." Except where indicated, my citations occur in these articles.
Davis believes that the notations were made in 1906; but some clearly were written
much earlier, and perhaps all were. Regardless, the markings show Clemens' reactions to Lecky's points. Paine does not cite the annotated edition which he has
seen, but quotes comments by Clemens differing from those which Davis cites.

At the outset Lecky notices that there are two fundamentally opposed groups of moralists:

> One of them is generally described as the stoical, the intuitive, the independent, and the sentimental; the other as the epicurean, the inductive, the utilitarian, or the selfish. The moralists of the former school . . . believe that we have a natural power of perceiving that some qualities such as benevolence, chastity, or veracity, are better than others, and that we ought to cultivate them, and to repress their opposites. . . . They contend, that by the constitution of our nature, the nature of right carries with it an obligation; that to say a course of conduct is our duty, is in itself, and apart from all consequences, an intelligible and sufficient reason for practicing it; and that we derive the first principles of our duty from intuition. The moralist of the opposite school denies that we have any such natural perception. He maintains that we have by nature absolutely no knowledge of merit and demerit, of the comparative excellence of our feelings and actions, and that we derive these notions solely from observation of the course . . . which is conducive to human happiness. That which makes actions good is, that they increase the happiness or diminish the pains of mankind. That which constitutes their demerit is the opposite tendency.

Lecky favored the intuitionists and wrote his history accordingly. In his survey of pagan philosophers he praises the Stoics for believing that "duty, as distinguished from every modification of selfishness, should be the supreme motive of life," and for abstaining from sin "not through fear of punishment" but "from the desire and obligation of what is just and good." Lecky notices that by contrast the populace urged men to be good so as to avoid punishment: "The Greek word for superstition signifies literally 'fear of the gods,' or daemons, and the philosophers sometimes represent the vulgar as shuddering at the thought of death, through dread of certain endless sufferings to which it would lead them." Clemens scored these passages.

Later, in "The Conversion of Rome," Lecky tells of the opposition of philosophers to early Christians because "'To agitate the minds of men with religious terrorism, to . . . govern the reason by alarming the imagination, was in the eyes of the Pagan world one of the most heinous of crimes." In the margin Clemens wrote: "It is an odious religion." Then (perhaps thinking of friends in the clergy) he added: "Still I do not think its priests ought to be burned, but only the missionaries."

Recalling the stern tenets of Calvinism according to which he had been reared and his later studies in science, and availing himself of help from De Quille, the humorist has Huck in chapter ii picture counterparts of Lecky's *hoi polloi* of antiquity and his noble Stoics in St. Petersburg. Miss Watson is the selfish philosopher who tries to make Huck behave by talking of "the bad place" and "the good place" and claiming he can get what he prays for. Widow Douglas—a noble Stoic—is one of Lecky's fellow intuitionists: "she said the thing a body could get by praying for it was 'spiritual gifts.' This was too much for me, but she told me what she meant—I must help other people, and do everything I could for other people, and look out for them all the time and never think about myself."

Huck weighs the formulas and like Lecky discovers a dichotomy:

> I went out in the woods and turned [the widow's recipe] over in my mind a long time—but I couldn't see no advantage about it—except for the other people—so at last I reckoned I wouldn't worry about it any more, but just let it go. Sometimes the widow would take me one side and talk about Providence in a way to make a body's mouth water; but maybe next day Miss Watson would take hold and knock it all down again. I judged I could see there was two Providences, and a poor chap would stand considerable show with the widow's Providence, but if Miss Watson's got him there warn't no help for him any more. I . . . reckoned I would belong to the widow's if he wanted me, though I couldn't make out how he was agoing to be any better off then than he was before, seeing I was so ignorant, and so kind of low-down and ornery.

Lecky would have considered Huck confused. The boy's natural power of perceiving (to use Lecky's term) makes him sense the superiority of the widow's moral scheme. But he talks like a utilitarian. For since he "can't see no advantages about" the widow's doctrine for himself, he selfishly decides to "let it go." And instead of seeing that he has innate ability to choose virtue, he figures that because he is "igno-rant, . . . low-down and ornery" (a matter that would concern only a "selfish" philosopher) he cannot be very good. Early in the book, then, under Lecky's stimulation, the author begins to contrast two moral philosophies which become increasingly important as the book progresses.[3]

Despite his enthusiasm about Lecky, the humorist agreed with Huck that environment determines morality. When Lecky remarked that in

---

[3] Without reference to Lecky, Edgar Marquess Branch, *The Literary Apprentice-ship of Mark Twain* (Urbana, 1950), pp. 200 ff., has pointed out the differences be-tween the widow's and Miss Watson's "providences." He has gone on to argue that this contrast initiates a theme running through the novel: "the main action may be interpreted as Huck's faltering progress toward the widow's providence. . . ." This hypothesis leads Branch to several valuable insights, though, as will be seen, I do not believe that it is completely sound.

different ages men had different ideas as to what was humane but that this fact provided no satisfactory argument against "the reality of innate moral perceptions," Clemens fiercely (and with satirical illogic) disagreed in a marginal comment: "All moral perceptions are acquired by the influences around us; these influences begin in infancy; we never get a chance to find out whether we have any that are innate or not." When Lecky praised Christianity for "quickening greatly our benevolent affections," beginning this influence "with the very earliest stage of human life," Clemens sneered in the margin, "And so nothing of it was innate."

In chapter viii, on agreeing not to report Jim has run away Huck shows how his moral standards are influenced by his upbringing by accepting the fact that "people would call me a low-down Abolitionist and despise me." This point had been made briefly in chapter xxviii of *Tom Sawyer*, where Huck had agreed with the popular view that he did wrong when he sat and ate with a Negro.[4]

The novelist also agreed with Lecky's opponents that selfish interests govern actions. Lecky paraphrases the philosophical views of Hobbes, Bentham, Mill, Locke, and their group thus: "A desire to obtain happiness and to avoid pain is the only possible motive to action. The reason, and the only reason, why we should perform virtuous actions, or . . . seek the good of others, is that on the whole such a course will bring us the greatest amount of happiness." Clemens underlined this, bracketed the "should," underscored "us," and commented: "Leave the 'should' out—then it is perfect (and true)." Paine's report that he wrote beside this passage "Sound and true"—if accurate—indicates that Clemens read and marked two copies of Lecky's book and twice agreed with Lecky's opponents at this very point.

Paine adds that when Lecky wrote that laws restrain our appetites, "being sustained by rewards and punishments . . . make it the interest of the individual to regard that of the community," Clemens wrote, "Correct! He has proceeded from unreasoned selfishness to reasoned selfishness. All our acts, reasoned and unreasoned, are selfish." Huck illustrates this in chapter xii. He invades farms to "borrow" a melon, corn, or other provisions. Pap had said borrowing things was not wrong "if you was going to pay them back some time but the widow said it warn't anything but a soft name for stealing, and no decent body would do it." Taking heed of the widow, Jim and Huck decide "to pick out two or three things from the list and say we won't borrow

4 A passage in Lecky which Clemens scored may have called his attention to this disparity between what was right and what the law sanctioned: in it Lecky notices "how widely the opinions of the philosophic classes in Rome were removed from the professed religion of the State" and that "the opinions of learned men never reflect faithfully those of the vulgar. . . ."

them no more," and award immunity to crabapples and persimmons. "I was glad the way it come out," says Huck, "because crabapples ain't ever good, and the p'simmons wouldn't be ripe for two or three months yet"—a neat instance of selfish interests shaping a moral decision.

Also illustrated is Lecky's point that when a man's conscience is active, "If happiness be his object, he must regulate his course with a view to the actual condition of his being, and there can be little doubt that his peace will be most promoted by a compromise with vice." [5] In chapter xvi the slave hunters make such a compromise. Persuaded by Huck that his family is suffering from smallpox, they refuse to help them but salve their consciences by giving Huck two twenty-dollar gold pieces.

Chapter xvi repeats other points. As Huck and Jim watch for Cairo, Huck is worried by Jim's talk of being freed: "it made me all over trembly and feverish . . . because I begun to get it through my head that he *was* most free—and who was to blame for it? Why, *me.*" To make the matter clearer, the author, when preparing readings from a personal copy of the book for a lecture some years later, made an addition which, like others, helps clarify his meaning. Here he inserted: "O, I had committed a *crime!*—I knowed it perfectly *well*—I could *see* it, *now.*" [6] As he has indicated in chapter viii, moral standards are made by the community. In chapter iii Huck, when he lies to help Jim, blames his own training: "I see it warn't no use for me to try to learn to do right; a body that don't get *started* right when he's little ain't got no show." And in the end Huck makes what appears to be a selfish decision.

It *appears* to be a selfish decision, but, along with a struggle which preceded it, the decision needs to be carefully examined. Chapter xvi is particularly interesting because, although in chapters xii and xv [7] Huck has recounted wrestling matches with his conscience, this chapter contains the most detailed account of such a battle in the 1876 chapters.

Again, reading Lecky and thinking about Lecky seem to have been instructive. The intuitive moralist, says Lecky, doubts that a man's conscience alone can make him do right; such a moralist "denies . . . that those pains and pleasures [which conscience affords] are so power-

5 Clemens did not mark this passage in I, 60-64, of his edition.

6 Copyright © 1960 by Mark Twain Co. Clemens' copy of the Tauchnitz edition, with his markings and insertions, is in Mark Twain Papers, University of California Library, Berkeley (hereafter *MTP*). Page references in Notebook 28a, kept between May 15, 1895, and August 23, 1895, *MTP*, indicate that this edition and the marked passages were used in lectures.

7 In chapter xii Huck and Jim make the decision about borrowing. Huck says, "We warn't feeling just right before that [decision], but it was all comfortable now." In chapter xvi, after fooling Jim, Huck spends fifteen minutes deciding to apologize. In neither instance, though, are the workings of conscience explored.

ful or so proportioned to our acts as to become an adequate basis for virtue." Also, whether virtue or vice wins, a man's conscience gives him trouble. If it prevents a man's sinning, "the suffering caused by resisting natural tendencies is much greater than will ensue from their moderate gratification." If the man sins, he "possesses a conscience . . . and its sting or approval constitutes a pain or a pleasure so intense, as to redress the balance." "And, indeed, on the whole," Lecky summarizes, "it is more than doubtful whether conscience . . . is not the cause of more pain than pleasure. Its reproaches are more felt than its approval." Anyone, therefore, who believes that "ought or ought not means nothing more than the prospect of acquiring or losing pleasure" should, Lecky suggests, simply get rid of his conscience: "That it would be for the happiness as it would certainly be in the power of a man of a temperament such as I have . . . described, to quench that conscientious feeling which by its painful reproaches prevents him from pursuing the course that would be most conducive to his tranquility, I conceive to be self-evident." [8]

Mark showed clearly that he agreed about the troublesomeness of conscience and the desirability of getting rid of the thing. He read to the Monday Evening Club, January 24, 1876, "The Facts Concerning the Recent Carnival of Crime in Connecticut," published in the *Atlantic Monthly* a month before he started to write *Huck.* In it a deformed dwarf covered with fuzzy green mould, a caricature of the author, visits Mark. This creature, with "a fox-like cunning in the face and the sharp little eyes, and also alertness and malice," reminds his host of past sins and tortures him with remorse:

> He reminded me of many dishonest things which I had done; . . . of some which I had planned . . . and been kept from performing by consequences only. . . . With exquisite cruelty he recalled to my mind . . . wrongs and unkindnesses I had inflicted and humiliations I had put upon friends since dead, "who died thinking of those injuries, maybe, and grieving over them," he added, by way of poison to the stab.

The shrunken creature is, he reveals, his own conscience. When he asks why all consciences are "nagging, badgering, fault-finding savages," the dwarf answers, "The *purpose* of it is to improve the man, but *we* are merely disinterested agents. . . . It is my *business*—and my joy—to make you repent of *every*thing you do." Gleefully following Lecky's suggestion, the narrator kills the troublesome dwarf and begins a life of crime:

> Nothing in all the world could persuade me to have a conscience again. . . . I killed thirty-eight persons during the first two weeks—all of them

---

8 Clemens did not mark these passages, I, 62-64, of the 1874 edition.

on account of ancient grudges. I burned a dwelling that interrupted my
view. I swindled a widow and some orphans out of their last cow, which
is a very good one, though not a thoroughbred, I believe. I have also committed scores of crimes, . . . and have enjoyed my work exceedingly,
whereas it would formerly have broken my heart and turned my hair
gray. . . .

This fantasy was particularly exuberant perhaps because an oversen-
sitive conscience long had tortured Clemens himself. Howells says,
"Among the half-dozen, or half-hundred personalities that each of us
becomes, I should say that Clemens's central and final personality
was something exquisite. . . . One could not know him well without
realizing him . . . the most conscientious of men." Rudyard Kipling
too noticed evidence of great sensitivity—"a mouth as delicate as a
woman's." [9] The author's *Autobiography* and his biographies are dotted
with instances of his suffering pangs of conscience. His own experiences
therefore helped him approve Lecky's thesis that a man's conscience
bedevils him whatever he does.

This belief led him, in chapter xvi, to have Huck suffer agonies because he is helping Jim escape. Here is the passage, with additions for
the reading bracketed:

. . . conscience up and says, every time, "But you knowed he was running
for his freedom, and you could a paddled ashore and told somebody."
That was so—[yes it was so—] I couldn't get around that, noway. . . .
Conscience says . . . "What had poor Miss Watson done to you, that you
could see her nigger go off right under your eyes and never say one
single word? What did that poor old woman do to you, that you should
treat her so mean? Why, she tried to learn you your book, she tried to
learn you your manners, [she tried to learn you to be a Christian],[10] she
tried to be good to you. . . ."
I got to feeling so mean and so miserable I most wished I was dead.

And Huck's decision to tell on Jim brings a fine feeling of relief: "[O,
it was a blessed thought! I never can *tell* how good it made me feel—
cuz I *knowed* I was doing *right*, now.] I felt easy and happy and light
as a feather right off. All my troubles was gone." Apparently, such
relief follows any decision, wrong or right. After deciding to refrain
from borrowing crabapples and persimmons, says Huck, "We warn't
feeling just right before that [decision], but it was all comfortable
now." Here Twain joins Lecky and other intuitionists in denying that

9 *My Mark Twain* (New York, 1910), p. 34; Kipling, *From Sea to Sea* (New York,
1913), II, 170.
10 All interpolated passages © copyright 1960 by Mark Twain Co.

"pains and pleasures" of conscience "are . . . so proportioned to our acts as to become an adequate basis for virtues."

Conscience pulls Huck equally hard the other way. As he paddles toward shore he hears Jim shout, "You's de bes' fren' Jim's ever had; en you's de *only* fren' ole Jim's got now."

> I was paddling off, all in a sweat to tell on him; but when he says this, it seemed to kind of take the tuck all out of me. [It kind of all *unsettled* me, and I couldn't seem to *tell* whether I was doing *right* or doing *wrong*.] I went along slow then, and I warn't right down certain whether I was glad I started or whether I warn't. When I was [100 and] fifty yards off, Jim [sings out across the darkness and] says:
> "Dah you goes, de ole true Huck; de on'y white genlman dat ever kep' his promise to old Jim."
> Well, I just felt sick.

Sick or not, Huck has decided "I *got* to do it," when two slave hunters appear and question him. He tries to tell the truth, "but I warn't man enough—hadn't the spunk of a rabbit." So he lies and saves Jim. Here is the aftermath:

> I got aboard the raft, feeling bad and low, because I knowed I had done wrong. . . . Then I thought a minute, and says to myself, hold on; s'pose you'd 'a' done right and give Jim up, would you feel better than what you do now? No, says I, I'd feel bad—I'd feel just the same way I do now. [As fur as I can see, a conscience is put in you just to *object* to whatever you *do* do, don't make no difference what it *is*.] Well, then, says I, what's the use you learning to do right, when it's troublesome to do right and ain't no trouble to do wrong, and the wages is just the same? I was stuck. So I reckoned I wouldn't bother no more about it, but after this always do whichever come handiest at the time.

Considered in the context of Clemens' argument with Lecky, this is a complex passage. Huck's decision that hereafter he will "do which-ever comes handiest at the time" seems to be a decision to do what is expedient. But if he acts as he does on this occasion, the expedient thing, for him, will be the humane thing. Thus he will confound Lecky; for, though acting expediently, he will reach the same sort of decision a noble intuitive philosopher would reach, and for the same reason.

But an interpolation in the text and a passage in a notebook which Clemens wrote for his lecture tour in 1895 show that another concept is involved. To Jim's shout about Huck's being his only friend he added, "O bless de good old heart o' you, Huck!" And in his notebook of 1895 he wrote a fascinating interpretation of this very passage. His plan, the notebook makes clear, was to "get up an elaborate and formal lay sermon on morals and the conduct of life, and things of that stately sort" [11] illustrated with readings. The introduction to this passage is quite explicit:

> Next, I should exploit the proposition that in a crucial moral emergency a sound heart is a safer guide than an ill-trained conscience. I sh'd support this doctrine with a chapter from a book of mine where a sound heart and a deformed conscience come into collision and conscience suffers defeat. Two persons figure in this chapter: Jim, a middle-aged slave, and Huck Finn, a boy of 14, . . . bosom friends, drawn together by a community of misfortune. . . .
>
> In those old slave-holding days the whole community was agreed as to one thing—the awful sacredness of slave property. To help steal a horse or a cow was a low crime, but to help a hunted slave . . . or hesitate to promptly betray him to a slave-catcher when opportunity offered was a much baser crime, and carried with it a stain, a moral smirch which nothing could wipe away. That this sentiment should exist among slave-holders is comprehensible—there were good commercial reasons for it—but that it should exist and did exist among the paupers . . . and in a passionate and uncompromising form, is not in our remote day realizable. It seemed natural enough to me then; natural enough that Huck and his father the worthless loafer should feel and approve it, though it seems now absurd. It shows that that strange thing, the conscience—that unerring monitor—can be trained to approve any wild thing you *want* it to approve if you begin its education early and stick to it.[12]

If Clemens here interpreted correctly a passage written nineteen years before, he had intended to distinguish between conscience, a person's sense of right and wrong developed by his community, and a sound heart—something innate closely resembling Lecky's "natural power." Huck's virtuous decision results from his heart's triumph over his conscience.

[11] Notebook 28a, TS p. 21, *MTP*, © copyright 1960 by Mark Twain Co.
[12] Notebook 28a, TS pp. 35-36, *MTP,* © copyright by Mark Twain Co.

A Sound Heart and a Deformed Conscience

by Henry Nash Smith

Mark Twain worked on *Adventures of Huckleberry Finn* at inter-
vals over a period of seven years, from 1876 to 1883. During this time
he wrote two considerable books (*A Tramp Abroad* and *The Prince
and the Pauper*), expanded "Old Times on the Mississippi" into *Life
on the Mississippi*, and gathered various shorter pieces into three other
volumes. But this is all essentially minor work. The main line of his
development lies in the long preoccupation with the Matter of Hannibal and the Matter of the River that is recorded in "Old Times"
and *The Adventures of Tom Sawyer* and reaches a climax in his book
about "Tom Sawyer's Comrade. Scene: The Mississippi Valley. Time:
Forty to Fifty Years Ago."

In writing *Huckleberry Finn* Mark Twain found a way to organize
into a larger structure the insights that earlier humorists had recorded
in their brief anecdotes.[1] This technical accomplishment was of course
inseparable from the process of discovering new meanings in his material. His development as a writer was a dialectic interplay in which the
reach of his imagination imposed a constant strain on his technical
resources, and innovations of method in turn opened up new vistas
before his imagination.

The dialectic process is particularly striking in the gestation of
Huckleberry Finn. The use of Huck as a narrative persona, with the
consequent elimination of the author as an intruding presence in the
story, resolved the difficulties about point of view and style that had
been so conspicuous in the earlier books. But turning the story over

"A Sound Heart and a Deformed Conscience" by *Henry Nash Smith*. From Mark
Twain: The Development of a Writer *(Cambridge: Harvard University Press, 1962),
pp. 113-23. Copyright © 1962 by the President and Fellows of Harvard College. Reprinted by permission of the Belknap Press of Harvard University Press. The essay
has been abridged for this volume.*

[1] This essay makes constant use of Walter Blair's impressive *Mark Twain & Huck
Finn* (Berkeley, 1960). But my reading of *Huckleberry Finn* has of course been influenced also by other books and articles. I should mention particularly chapter 15 in
Daniel G. Hoffman's *Form and Fable in American Fiction* (New York, 1961), which
deals expertly with the folklore in the novel.

to Huck brought into view previously unsuspected literary potentiali-
ties in the vernacular perspective, particularly the possibility of using
vernacular speech for serious purposes and of transforming the vernacular narrator from a mere persona into a character with human
depth. Mark Twain's response to the challenge made *Huckleberry Finn*
the greatest of his books and one of the two or three acknowledged
masterpieces of American literature. Yet this triumph created a new
technical problem to which there was no solution; for what had begun
as a comic story developed incipiently tragic implications contradicting
the premises of comedy.

Huckleberry Finn thus contains three main elements. The most conspicuous is the story of Huck's and Jim's adventures in their flight
toward freedom. Jim is running away from actual slavery, Huck from
the cruelty of his father, from the well-intentioned "sivilizing" efforts
of Miss Watson and the Widow Douglas, from respectability and rou-
tine in general. The second element in the novel is social satire of the
towns along the river. The satire is often transcendently funny, especially in episodes involving the rascally Duke and King, but it can also
deal in appalling violence, as in the Grangerford-Shepherdson feud or
Colonel Sherburn's murder of the helpless Boggs. The third major
element in the book is the developing characterization of Huck.

All three elements must have been present to Mark Twain's mind
in some sense from the beginning, for much of the book's greatness
lies in its basic coherence, the complex interrelation of its parts. Nevertheless, the intensive study devoted to it in recent years, particularly
Walter Blair's establishment of the chronology of its composition,[2] has
demonstrated that Mark Twain's search for a structure capable of doing justice to his conceptions of theme and character passed through
several stages. He did not see clearly where he was going when he began to write, and we can observe him in the act of making discoveries
both in meaning and in method as he goes along.

The narrative tends to increase in depth as it moves from the adventure story of the early chapters into the social satire of the long
middle section, and thence to the ultimate psychological penetration
of Huck's character in the moral crisis of Chapter 31. Since the crisis
is brought on by the shock of the definitive failure of Huck's effort
to help Jim, it marks the real end of the quest for freedom. The per-
plexing final sequence on the Phelps plantation is best regarded as a
maneuver by which Mark Twain beats his way back from incipient
tragedy to the comic resolution called for by the original conception
of the story.

2 "When Was *Huckleberry Finn* Written?" *American Literature,* XXX (March,
1958), 1-25.

II

Huck's and Jim's flight from St. Petersburg obviously translates into action the theme of vernacular protest. The fact that they have no means of fighting back against the forces that threaten them but can only run away is accounted for in part by the conventions of backwoods humor, in which the inferior social status of the vernacular character placed him in an ostensibly weak position. But it also reflects Mark Twain's awareness of his own lack of firm ground to stand on in challenging the established system of values.

Huck's and Jim's defenselessness foreshadows the outcome of their efforts to escape. They cannot finally succeed. To be sure, in a superficial sense they do succeed; at the end of the book Jim is technically free and Huck still has the power to light out for the Territory. But Jim's freedom has been brought about by such an implausible device that we do not believe in it. Who can imagine the scene in which Miss Watson decides to liberate him? What were her motives? Mark Twain finesses the problem by placing this crucial event far offstage and telling us nothing about it beyond the bare fact he needs to resolve his plot. And the notion that a fourteen-year-old boy could make good his escape beyond the frontier is equally unconvincing. The writer himself did not take it seriously. In an unpublished sequel to *Huckleberry Finn* called "Huck Finn and Tom Sawyer among the Indians," which he began soon after he finished the novel, Aunt Sally takes the boys and Jim back to Hannibal and then to western Missouri for a visit "with some of her relations on a hemp farm out there." Here Tom revives the plan mentioned near the end of *Huckleberry Finn:* he "was dead set on having us run off, some night, and cut for the Injun country and go for adventures." Huck says, however, that he and Jim "kind of hung fire. Plenty to eat and nothing to do. We was very well satisfied." Only after an extended debate can Tom persuade them to set out with him. Their expedition falls into the stereotyped pattern of Wild West stories of travel out the Oregon Trail, makes a few gibes at Cooper's romanticized Indians, and breaks off.³

The difficulty of imagining a successful outcome for Huck's and Jim's quest had troubled Mark Twain almost from the beginning of his work on the book. After writing the first section in 1876 he laid aside his manuscript near the end of Chapter 16.⁴ The narrative plan with which he had impulsively begun had run into difficulties. When

³ The story is preserved in the form of galley proof of type set by the Paige machine, DV 303, Mark Twain Papers. Quotations © copyright 1962 by the Mark Twain Company.

⁴ *Mark Twain & Huck Finn,* p. 151.

Huck and Jim shove off from Jackson's Island on their section of a lumber raft (at the end of Chapter 11) they do so in haste, to escape the immediate danger of the slave hunters Huck has learned about from Mrs. Loftus. No long-range plan is mentioned until the beginning of Chapter 15, when Huck says that at Cairo they intended to "sell the raft and get on a steamboat and go way up the Ohio amongst the free states, and then be out of trouble." [5] But they drift past Cairo in the fog, and a substitute plan of making their way back up to the mouth of the Ohio in their canoe is frustrated when the canoe disappears while they are sleeping: "we talked about what we better do, and found there warn't no way but just to go along down with the raft till we got a chance to buy a canoe to go back in." [6] Drifting downstream with the current, however, could not be reconciled with the plan to free Jim by transporting him up the Ohio; hence the temporary abandonment of the story.

III

When Mark Twain took up his manuscript again in 1879, after an interval of three years, he had decided upon a different plan for the narrative. Instead of concentrating on the story of Huck's and Jim's escape, he now launched into a satiric description of the society of the prewar South. Huck was essential to this purpose, for Mark Twain meant to view his subject ironically through Huck's eyes. But Jim was more or less superfluous. During Chapters 17 and 18, devoted to the Grangerford household and the feud, Jim has disappeared from the story. Mark Twain had apparently not yet found a way to combine social satire with the narrative scheme of Huck's and Jim's journey on the raft.

While he was writing his chapter about the feud, however, he thought of a plausible device to keep Huck and Jim floating southward while he continued his panoramic survey of the towns along the river. The device was the introduction of the Duke and the King. In Chapter 19 they come aboard the raft, take charge at once, and hold Huck and Jim in virtual captivity. In this fashion the narrative can preserve the overall form of a journey down the river while providing ample opportunity for satire when Huck accompanies the two rascals on their forays ashore. But only the outward form of the journey is retained. Its meaning has changed, for Huck's and Jim's quest for freedom has in effect come to an end. Jim is physically present but he assumes an entirely passive role, and is hidden with the raft for considerable periods. Huck is also essentially passive; his function now

[5] *Writings* (Definitive Edition, New York, 1922-25), XIII, 112.
[6] *Writings*, XIII, 130.

is that of an observer. Mark Twain postpones acknowledging that the quest for freedom has failed, but the issue will have to be faced eventually.

The satire of the towns along the banks insists again and again that the dominant culture is decadent and perverted. Traditional values have gone to seed. The inhabitants can hardly be said to live a conscious life of their own; their actions, their thoughts, even their emotions are controlled by an outworn and debased Calvinism, and by a residue of the eighteenth-century cult of sensibility. With few exceptions they are mere bundles of tropisms, at the mercy of scoundrels like the Duke and the King who know how to exploit their prejudices and delusions.

The falseness of the prevalent values finds expression in an almost universal tendency of the townspeople to make spurious claims to status through self-dramatization. Mark Twain has been concerned with this topic from the beginning of the book. Chapter 1 deals with Tom Sawyer's plan to start a band of robbers which Huck will be allowed to join only if he will "go back to the widow and be respectable"; [7] and we also hear about Miss Watson's mercenary conception of prayer. In Chapter 2 Jim interprets Tom's prank of hanging his hat on the limb of a tree while he is asleep as evidence that he has been bewitched. He "was most ruined for a servant, because he got stuck up on account of having seen the devil and been rode by witches." [8] Presently we witness the ritual by which Pap Finn is to be redeemed from drunkenness. When his benefactor gives him a lecture on temperance, it will be recalled,

> the old man cried, and said he'd been a fool, and fooled away his life; but now he was a-going to turn over a new leaf and be a man nobody wouldn't be ashamed of, and he hoped the judge would help him and not look down on him. The judge said he could hug him for them words; so *he* cried, and his wife she cried again; pap said he'd been a man that had always been misunderstood before, and the judge said he believed it. The old man said that what a man wanted that was down was sympathy, and the judge said it was so; so they cried again.[9]

As comic relief for the feud that provides a way of life for the male Grangerfords Mark Twain dwells lovingly on Emmeline Grangerford's pretensions to culture—her paintings with the fetching titles and the ambitious "Ode to Stephen Dowling Bots, Dec'd.," its pathos hopelessly flawed by the crudities showing through like the chalk beneath

[7] *Writings,* XIII, 2.
[8] *Writings,* XIII, 9.
[9] *Writings,* XIII, 30.

the enameled surface of the artificial fruit in the parlor: "His spirit was gone for to sport aloft/In the realms of the good and great." [10]

The Duke and the King personify the theme of fraudulent role-taking. These rogues are not even given names apart from the wildly improbable identities they assume in order to dominate Huck and Jim. The Duke's poses have a literary cast, perhaps because of the scraps of bombast he remembers from his experience as an actor. The illiterate King has "done considerable in the doctoring way," but when we see him at work it is mainly at preaching, "workin' camp-meetin's, and missionaryin' around." [11] Pretended or misguided piety and other perversions of Christianity obviously head the list of counts in Mark Twain's indictment of the prewar South. And properly: for it is of course religion that stands at the center of the system of values in the society of this fictive world and by implication in all societies. His revulsion, expressed through Huck, reaches its highest pitch in the scene where the King delivers his masterpiece of "soul-butter and hog-wash" for the benefit of the late Peter Wilks's fellow townsmen.

> By and by the king he gets up and comes forward a little, and works himself up and slobbers out a speech, all full of tears and flapdoodle, about its being a sore trial for him and his poor brother to lose the diseased, and to miss seeing diseased alive after the long journey of four thousand mile, but it's a trial that's sweetened and sanctified to us by this dear sympathy and these holy tears, and so he thanks them out of his heart and out of his brother's heart, because out of their mouths they can't, words being too weak and cold, and all that kind of rot and slush, till it was just sickening; and then he blubbers out a pious goody-goody Amen, and turns himself loose and goes to crying fit to bust.[12]

IV

Huck is revolted by the King's hypocrisy: "I never see anything so disgusting." He has had a similar reaction to the brutality of the feud: "It made me so sick I most fell out of the tree." [13] In describing such scenes he speaks as moral man viewing an immoral society, an observer who is himself free of the vices and even the weaknesses he describes. Mark Twain's satiric method requires that Huck be a mask for the writer, not a fully developed character. The method has great ironic force, and is in itself a technical landmark in the history of American fiction, but it prevents Mark Twain from doing full justice to Huck

---

10 *Writings,* XIII, 143.
11 *Writings,* XIII, 169.
12 *Writings,* XIII, 227-28.
13 *Writings,* XIII, 160.

as a person in his own right, capable of mistakes in perception and judgment, troubled by doubts and conflicting impulses.

Even in the chapters written during the original burst of composition in 1876 the character of Huck is shown to have depths and complexities not relevant to the immediate context. Huck's and Jim's journey down the river begins simply as a flight from physical danger; and the first episodes of the voyage have little bearing on the novelistic possibilities in the strange comradeship between outcast boy and escaped slave. But in Chapter 15, when Huck plays a prank on Jim by persuading him that the separation in the fog was only a dream, Jim's dignified and moving rebuke suddenly opens up a new dimension in the relation. Huck's humble apology is striking evidence of growth in moral insight. It leads naturally to the next chapter in which Mark Twain causes Huck to face up for the first time to the fact that he is helping a slave to escape. It is as if the writer himself were discovering unsuspected meanings in what he had thought of as a story of picaresque adventure. The incipient contradiction between narrative plan and increasing depth in Huck's character must have been as disconcerting to Mark Twain as the difficulty of finding a way to account for Huck's and Jim's continuing southward past the mouth of the Ohio. It was doubtless the convergence of the two problems that led him to put aside the manuscript near the end of Chapter 16.[14]

The introduction of the Duke and the King not only took care of the awkwardness in the plot but also allowed Mark Twain to postpone the exploration of Huck's moral dilemma. If Huck is not a free agent he is not responsible for what happens and is spared the agonies of choice. Throughout the long middle section, while he is primarily an observer, he is free of inner conflict because he is endowed by implication with Mark Twain's own unambiguous attitude toward the fraud and folly he witnesses.

In Chapter 31, however, Huck escapes from his captors and faces once again the responsibility for deciding on a course of action. His situation is much more desperate than it had been at the time of his first struggle with his conscience. The raft has borne Jim hundreds of miles downstream from the pathway of escape and the King has turned him over to Silas Phelps as a runaway slave. The quest for freedom has "all come to nothing, everything all busted up and ruined." [15] Huck thinks of notifying Miss Watson where Jim is, since if he must be a slave he would be better off "at home where his family was." But

---

14 In *Mark Twain and Southwestern Humor* (Boston, 1959, pp. 216-19) Kenneth Lynn points out that Mark Twain's dawning recognition of moral depth in Huck's character created a difficulty for him at this point. Mr. Lynn's analysis has led me to modify my earlier view of the problem of plot construction in the novel.

15 *Writings*, XIII, 294.

then Huck realizes that Miss Watson would probably sell Jim down the river as a punishment for running away. Furthermore, Huck himself would be denounced by everyone for his part in the affair. In this fashion his mind comes back once again to the unparalleled wickedness of acting as accomplice in a slave's escape.

The account of Huck's mental struggle in the next two or three pages is the emotional climax of the story. It draws together the theme of flight from bondage and the social satire of the middle section, for Huck is trying to work himself clear of the perverted value system of St. Petersburg. Both adventure story and satire, however, are now subordinate to an exploration of Huck's psyche which is the ultimate achievement of the book. The issue is identical with that of the first moral crisis, but the later passage is much more intense and richer in implication. The differences appear clearly if the two crises are compared in detail.

In Chapter 16 Huck is startled into a realization of his predicament when he hears Jim, on the lookout for Cairo at the mouth of the Ohio, declare that "he'd be a free man the minute he seen it, but if he missed it he'd be in a slave country again and no more show for freedom." Huck says: "I begun to get it through my head that he *was* most free— and who was to blame for it? Why, *me.* I couldn't get that out of my conscience, no how nor no way." He dramatizes his inner debate by quoting the words in which his conscience denounces him: "What had poor Miss Watson done to you that you could see her nigger go off right under your eyes and never say one single word? What did that poor old woman do to you that you could treat her so mean? Why, she tried to learn you your book, she tried to learn you your manners, she tried to be good to you every way she knowed how. *That's* what she done." The counterargument is provided by Jim, who seems to guess what is passing through Huck's mind and does what he can to invoke the force of friendship and gratitude: "Pooty soon I'll be a-shout'n' for joy, en I'll say, it's all on accounts o' Huck; I's a free man, en I couldn't ever ben free ef it hadn' ben for Huck; Huck done it. Jim won't ever forget you, Huck; you's de bes' fren' Jim's ever had; en you's de *only* fren' ole Jim's got now." Huck nevertheless sets out for the shore in the canoe "all in a sweat to tell on" Jim, but when he is intercepted by the two slave hunters in a skiff he suddenly contrives a cunning device to ward them off. We are given no details about how his inner conflict was resolved.[16]

In the later crisis Huck provides a much more circumstantial account of what passes through his mind. He is now quite alone; the outcome of the debate is not affected by any stimulus from the outside. It is the memory of Jim's kindness and goodness rather than Jim's actual voice that impels Huck to defy his conscience: "I see Jim before me all the time: in the day and in the night-time, sometimes moonlight, sometimes storms, and we a-floating along, talking and singing and laughing." [17] The most striking feature of this later crisis is the fact that Huck's conscience, which formerly had employed only secular arguments, now deals heavily in religious cant:

> At last, when it hit me all of a sudden that here was the plain hand of Providence slapping me in the face and letting me know my wickedness was being watched all the time from up there in heaven, whilst I was stealing a poor old woman's nigger that hadn't ever done me no harm, and now was showing me there's One that's always on the lookout, and ain't a-going to allow no such miserable doings to go only just so fur and no further, I most dropped in my tracks I was so scared.[18]

In the earlier debate the voice of Huck's conscience is quoted directly, but the bulk of the later exhortation is reported in indirect discourse. This apparently simple change in method has remarkable consequences. According to the conventions of first-person narrative, the narrator functions as a neutral medium in reporting dialogue. He remembers the speeches of other characters but they pass through his mind without affecting him. When Huck's conscience speaks within quotation marks it is in effect a character in the story, and he is not responsible for what it says. But when he paraphrases the admonitions of his conscience they are incorporated into his own discourse. Thus although Huck is obviously remembering the bits of theological jargon from sermons justifying slavery, they have become a part of his vocabulary.

The device of having Huck paraphrase rather than quote the voice of conscience may have been suggested to Mark Twain by a discovery he made in revising Huck's report of the King's address to the mourners in the Wilks parlor (Chapter 25).[19] The manuscript version of the passage shows that the King's remarks were composed as a direct quotation, but in the published text they have been put, with a minimum of verbal change, into indirect discourse. The removal of the barrier of quotation marks brings Huck into much more intimate contact with the King's "rot and slush" despite the fact that the paraphrase quivers with disapproval. The voice of conscience speaks in the precise accents

[17] *Writings,* XIII, 296.
[18] *Writings,* XIII, 294-95.
[19] Mr. Blair called to my attention the revision of this passage.

of the King but Huck is now completely uncritical. He does not question its moral authority; it is morality personified. The greater subtlety of the later passage illustrates the difference between the necessarily shallow characterization of Huck while he was being used merely as a narrative persona, and the profound insight which Mark Twain eventually brought to bear on his protagonist.

The recognition of complexity in Huck's character enabled Mark Twain to do full justice to the conflict between vernacular values and the dominant culture. By situating in a single consciousness both the perverted moral code of a society built on slavery and the vernacular commitment to freedom and spontaneity, he was able to represent the opposed perspectives as alternative modes of experience for the same character. In this way he gets rid of the confusions surrounding the pronoun "I" in the earlier books, where it sometimes designates the author speaking in his own person, sometimes an entirely distinct fictional character. Furthermore, the insight that enabled him to recognize the conflict between accepted values and vernacular protest as a struggle within a single mind does justice to its moral depth, whereas the device he had used earlier—in *The Innocents Abroad,* for example —of identifying the two perspectives with separate characters had flattened the issue out into melodrama. The satire of a decadent slaveholding society gains immensely in force when Mark Twain demonstrates that even the outcast Huck has been in part perverted by it. Huck's conscience is simply the attitudes he has taken over from his environment. What is still sound in him is an impulse from the deepest level of his personality that struggles against the overlay of prejudice and false valuation imposed on all members of the society in the name of religion, morality, law, and refinement.

Finally, it should be pointed out that the conflict in Huck between generous impulse and false belief is depicted by means of a contrast between colloquial and exalted styles. In moments of crisis his conscience addresses him in the language of the dominant culture, a tawdry and faded effort at a high style that is the rhetorical equivalent of the ornaments in the Grangerford parlor. Yet speaking in dialect does not in itself imply moral authority. By every external criterion the King is as much a vernacular character as Huck. The conflict in which Huck is involved is not that of a lower against an upper class or of an alienated fringe of outcasts against a cultivated elite. It is not the issue of frontier West versus genteel East, or of backwoods versus metropolis, but of fidelity to the uncoerced self versus the blurring of attitudes caused by social conformity, by the effort to achieve status or power through exhibiting the approved forms of sensibility.

The exploration of Huck's personality carried Mark Twain beyond satire and even beyond his statement of a vernacular protest against the dominant culture into essentially novelistic modes of writing. Some of the passages he composed when he got out beyond his polemic framework challenge comparison with the greatest achievements in the world's fiction.

Southwestern Vernacular

by James M. Cox

To say that in *Huckleberry Finn* Mark Twain extended his humor into serious territory is not to say that his humor became serious, but that larger areas of seriousness came under the dominion of his humor. If the turning of serious issues into the form of humor was the substantial inversion of the book, the formal inversion lay in transforming dialect into vernacular, which is to say making it the vehicle of vision. In terms of literary history, *Huckleberry Finn* marks the full emergence of an American language, and although Mark Twain did not accomplish the process alone, he *realized* the tradition which he inherited. The "Southwest" humorists—Hooper, Longstreet, Harris, and Thorpe; the comic journalists—Artemus Ward, Petroleum V. Nasby, Josh Billings, and John Phoenix; and the local colorists—Harriet Beecher Stowe, Bret Harte, Mary E. Wilkins Freeman, and Sarah Orne Jewett—had all used dialect. Yet in the humor of the old Southwest and in the literary achievements of the local colorists, the dialect was framed by a literary language which invariably condescended to it. The comic journalists, though they dropped the literary frame to appear as "characters," reduced dialect to a comic image. If the Southwest humorists tended to brutalize dialect characters and local colorists to sentimentalize them, the comic journalists, by reducing themselves to dialect, sought to give pungency and quaintness to conventional thought.

But something altogether different happens in *Huckleberry Finn*. The language is neither imprisoned in a frame nor distorted into a caricature; rather, it becomes a way of casting character and experience at the same time. This combination is the fine economy of Huckleberry Finn's style. Thus when Huck declares at the outset that he, not Mark Twain, will write this book, the language at one and the same time defines character and action.

"Southwestern Vernacular" by James M. Cox. From Mark Twain: The Fate of Humor *(Princeton: Princeton University Press, 1966), pp. 167-84. Copyright © 1966 by Princeton University Press. Reprinted by permission of the publisher. The essay has been abridged for this volume.*

You don't know about me without you have read a book by the name of
The Adventures of Tom Sawyer; but that ain't no matter. That book
was made by Mr. Mark Twain, and he told the truth, mainly. There was
things which he stretched, but mainly he told the truth. That is nothing.
I never seen anybody but lied one time or another, without it was Aunt
Polly, or the Widow, or maybe Mary. Aunt Polly—Tom's Aunt Polly,
she is—and Mary, and the Widow Douglas is all told about in that book,
which is mostly a true book, with some stretchers, as I said before.[1]

Nothing more seems to be going on here than in previous uses of
dialect. But by allowing Huck's vernacular merely to *imply* the literary form, Mark Twain was reorganizing the entire value system of
language, for all values had to be transmitted directly or indirectly
through Huck's vernacular. In turning the narration over to Huck,
Mark Twain abandoned the explicit norms and risked making his
vernacular force the reader to supply the implied norms. The vernacular he developed created the means of control within the reader's mind,
chiefly in three ways. First of all, Huck's incorrect language implied
standard, correct, literary English. Second, Huck's status as a child
invited an indulgence from the reader. Finally, Huck's action in time
and place—freeing a slave in the Old South before the Civil War—
insured moral approval from the reader. Though he is being a bad boy
in his own time, he is being a good boy in the reader's imagination.

All these controls, which are really *conventions,* exist outside the
novel. They are just what the style of the novel is *not;* for the style is
the inversion which implies the conventions yet remains their opposite.
And this style is Mark Twain's revolution in language, his rebellion in
form; and it marks the emergence of the American language to which
both Hemingway and Faulkner allude when they say that Mark Twain
was the first American writer, the writer from whom they descend.[2]

The freeing of the vernacular from the conventions is the larger
historical fact of form which provides an index to the action of the
novel. For this vernacular language, which implies respectable language, is not only the form of the book; it is at one and the same time
the character of Huckleberry Finn. To talk about the revolt of the
one should be to talk about the revolt of the other. I say *should,* because Huck's revolt seems on the face of things a genuinely tame performance. He is involved in a subversive project which has the reader's
complete approval—the freeing of a slave in the Old South, a world

---

1 *Writings* (Author's National Edition, New York, 1907-18), XIII, 1.
2 Hemingway's words were: "All modern American literature comes from one
book by Mark Twain called *Huckleberry Finn* . . . it's the best book we've had. All
American writing comes from that. There was nothing before. There has been nothing as good since" (*Green Hills of Africa* [New York, 1935], p. 22).

which, by virtue of the Civil War, has been declared morally reprehensible because of the slavery it condoned. Huck's rebellion is therefore being negotiated in a society which the reader's conscience indicts as morally wrong and which history has declared legally wrong. Moreover, Huck is a boy, a relatively harmless figure who drifts helplessly into his rebellion, making his subversion not only an act which the reader can approve but can indulge. His badness is inverted into goodness.

All this seems obvious, yet many readers never cease to celebrate the pluck of Huck's rebellion, when if this were all there was to it we would have nothing but the blandest sentimental action. What, after all, was courageous about writing in Hartford twenty years after the Civil War—or what is courageous about reading in a post-Civil War world—a book about a boy who was helping a slave to freedom? Such an act would be roughly equivalent to writing a novel in our time about a boy in Hitler's Germany helping a Jew to the border. Not that a great novel could not emerge from either of these subjects. In the case of *Huckleberry Finn* one did. Yet the boldness of the book—its exploration and discovery—does not reside in so tame a representation, but in the utilization of the action to gain the reader's assent to make the voyage downstream.

This built-in approval, stemming from Huck's initial "moral" advantage and from his being a boy—and thus evocative of the indulgent nostalgia Mark Twain had learned to exploit in *Tom Sawyer*—is what I take to be the "moral sentiment" of the book. But this moral sentiment is not the action of the book any more than the implicit conventional language is the style of the book. Rather, Huck's action is the inversion of the sentiment.

The humor of the book rides upon and at the same time requires this crucial inversion. For the more Huck berates himself for doing "bad" things, the more the reader approves him for doing "good" ones. Thus what for Huck is his worst action—refusing to turn Jim in to Miss Watson—is for the reader his best. When Huck says "All right, then, I'll *go* to hell," the reader is sure he is going to heaven. If this ironic relationship should ever break down, Huck's whole stature would be threatened. If Huck ever begins to think he is doing a good thing by helping Jim, he will become a good boy like Sid—one knowingly engaged in virtuous action; or a bad boy like Tom—one who can seem to go against society because he really knows that he is doing right. Clear though all this should be, the moral sentiment implied by the style inexorably arouses a wish that Huck have some recognition of his achievement.

It is just this wish which the ending of the novel frustrates; and since the wish is so pervasively exploited by the action of the novel, it is no wonder that the ending has been not a small problem. Of course, defenses of the ending can be made and have been made, but the point remains that they are defenses. No matter how adroit the critic, he begins from a position of special pleading, as if he were trying to convince himself that in an acknowledged masterpiece there could not really be such a wanton collapse. Even the most sympathetic critics of Mark Twain find the wiser path is to regret the closing ten chapters. Thus, Ernest Hemingway, after observing that modern American literature stemmed from *Huckleberry Finn,* went on to say, "If you read it you must stop where the Nigger Jim is stolen from the boys. That is the real end. The rest is just cheating." [3] Philip Young, following Hemingway, has gone so far as to declare that the beginning as well as the end could well be omitted without substantially taking away from the book.[4] So passionate an admirer of the book as Bernard De-Voto acknowledged that Mark Twain lost his purpose at the end and drifted into "inharmonious burlesque":

> A few pages earlier he had written the scene in which many readers have found his highest reach . . . And now, without any awareness that he was muddying the waters of great fiction, he plunges into a trivial extravaganza on a theme he had exhausted years before. In the whole reach of the English novel there is no more abrupt or more chilling descent.[5]

Probably the most formidable attack ever made on the ending of the book is found in Leo Marx's extremely interesting essay, "Mr. Eliot, Mr. Trilling, and *Huckleberry Finn.*" Exposing Trilling's and Eliot's rather perfunctory and evasive approvals of the ending, Marx presents a rigorous analysis of Mark Twain's failure in the closing chapters of his masterpiece. Mark Twain failed, Marx believes, because he refused the responsibilities which went with the vision of the journey. For the journey was, according to Marx, the Quest—the great voyage toward freedom which Huck and Jim had so precariously made. But in the last ten chapters, Marx feels that Mark Twain simply turns the book over to the high jinks of Tom Sawyer, while Huck shrinkingly assumes the stature of a little straight man, observing the burlesque antics of his companion, but apparently unmoved by them. The cause of this slump on Mark Twain's part, Marx concludes, is simply that the journey, the Quest, *cannot* succeed. The drifting river has taken

3 *Ibid.*
4 Philip Young, *Ernest Hemingway* (New York, 1952), p. 196.
5 Bernard DeVoto, *Mark Twain at Work* (Cambridge, Mass., 1942), p. 92.

Huck and Jim ever deeper into slavery, and Mark Twain, unable to resolve the paradox of this reality which defeats his wish, simply evades the entire issue by shifting to burlesque.[6]

Persuasive though this argument is, Mark Twain's form rules out the possibilities which Marx insists on. Since Huck's entire identity is based upon an inverted order of values just as his style is based upon "incorrect" usage, he cannot have any recognition of his own virtue. Failure to acknowledge this necessity causes Marx to see the journey as a quest, whereas it simply is not at any time a quest. A quest is a positive journey, implying an effort, a struggle to reach a goal. But Huck is escaping. His journey is primarily a negation, a flight *from* tyranny, not a flight toward freedom.

In fact, Huck's central mode of being is that of escape and evasion. He forgets much more than he remembers; he lies, steals, and in general participates in as many confidence tricks as the King and the Duke. But the two cardinal facts—that he is a boy and is involved in helping a runaway slave—serve endlessly to sustain the reader's approval. It is precisely this approval which, putting the reader's moral censor to sleep, provides the central good humor pervading the incongruities, absurdities, and cruelties through which the narrative beautifully makes its way. The vernacular inversion, which so surely evokes the feeling of approval and indulgence, is narratively embodied in the very drift of the great river on which the raft miraculously rides.[7]

To be sure, at the fateful moment when Huck determines to set Jim free, he finds himself in open rebellion against Negro slavery. But he comes reluctantly, not gloriously, forward; even as he makes his famous declaration to go to hell, he is looking for a way out. He is certainly not a rebel; he is in a tight place and does the *easiest* thing. The role of Abolitionist is not comfortable nor comforting to him and in turning over to Tom Sawyer the entire unpleasant business of freeing Jim, Huck is surely not acting out of but remarkably *in* character.

Marx's inversion of Huck's escape into a quest drives him to the position of saying that Mark Twain could not "acknowledge the truth his novel contained" and thus evaded the central moral responsibilities of his vision. Yet for Marx the "truth" amounts to nothing more

---

[6] Leo Marx, "Mr. Eliot, Mr. Trilling, and *Huckleberry Finn,*" *American Scholar,* XXII (Autumn, 1953), 423-40.

[7] The perfect integration between this drift and the river's motion is in part responsible for the beautiful economy with which Mark Twain treats the river. Far from needing to provide extensive descriptions and facts about the river as he did in *Life on the Mississippi,* he was able to render the river enormously real with economy of means. The reason: the fugitive boy and the river are made one through Huck's language.

than Huck's perceiving that Negro slavery is wrong and involving himself in a quest for *political* freedom. In saying that the ending of the book discloses a failure of nerve and a retreat to the genteel tradition, it seems to me that Marx is completely turned around. Surely the genteel Bostonians would have applauded the moral sentiment of antislavery and political freedom which the novel entertains. They would have welcomed the quest rather than the escape. Yet if Marx is wrong, what is there to say about the ending?

To begin with, the ending is, to use Huck's term, uncomfortable. The problem is to define the source of this discomfort. Without question, there is a change when Tom Sawyer reappears. The narrative movement changes from one of adventure to burlesque—a burlesque which, in place of Huck's sincere but helpless involvement in freeing a real slave, puts Tom Sawyer's relatively cruel yet successful lark of freeing a slave already free. It is not Mark Twain's failure to distinguish between the two actions which jeopardizes his book; rather, it is his ironic exposure of Tom's action which threatens the humor of the book and produces the inharmonious burlesque DeVoto regrets. Tom appears in such an unfortunate light in the closing pages that many readers of *Huckleberry Finn* can never again read *Tom Sawyer* without in one way or another holding Tom responsible for motives he had not had in the earlier book.

Tom's play seems unpardonable because he already knows that Jim is free. Yet this knowledge—which Tom withholds from Huck—finally clears up for Huck the mystery of Tom's behavior toward him. Upon at last discovering the knowledge Tom has withheld from him, Huck, who has been troubled by Tom's "badness," at last understands why his respectable companion has been able to commit such a crime. His only remaining problem is to find out why Tom spent so much effort "setting a free nigger free." This, too, is cleared up when Tom explains to the long-suffering Aunt Sally that he made his elaborate and vexing arrangements purely for "adventure."

Tom's adventures are a unique cruelty in a book which depicts so much cruelty. All the other cruelties are committed for some "reason" —for honor, money, or power. But Tom's cruelty has a purity all its own—it is done solely for the sake of adventure. After facing Tom's long play, it is possible to see Huck's famous remark about the King and the Duke in a larger perspective. "Human beings *can* be awful cruel to one another," Huck had said upon seeing the scoundrels ridden out of town on a rail. This statement not only points backward to the episodes with the King and the Duke, but serves as a gateway leading from the King and the Duke's departure to Tom Sawyer's performance. For Tom's pure play runs directly counter to a wish the journey has generated. That is the frustration of the ending—the inversion. Having felt Huck's slow discovery of Jim's humanity, the reader perforce deplores Tom's casual ignorance and unawareness.

Yet the judgment which the last ten chapters render upon Tom is surely the judgment rendered upon the moral sentiment on which the book has ridden. If the reader sees in Tom's performance a rather shabby and safe bit of play, he is seeing no more than the exposure of the approval with which he watched Huck operate. For if Tom is rather contemptibly setting a free slave free, what after all is the reader doing, who begins the book after the *fact* of the Civil War? This is the "joke" of the book—the moment when, in outrageous burlesque, it attacks the sentiment which its style has at once evoked and exploited. To see that Tom is doing at the ending what we have been doing throughout the book is essential to understanding what the book has meant to us. For when Tom proclaims to the assembled throng who have witnessed his performance that Jim "is as free as any cretur that walks this earth," he is an exposed embodiment of the complacent moral sentiment on which the reader has relied throughout the book. And to the extent the reader has indulged the complacency he will be disturbed by the ending.

To be frustrated by the ending is to begin to discover the meaning of this journey, which evokes so much indulgence and moral approval that the censor is put to sleep. Beneath the sleeping censor, the real rebellion of *Huckleberry Finn* is enacted. For there must be a real rebellion—a rebellion which cannot so easily be afforded—else Mark Twain is guilty of a failure far greater than the ending. If the "incorrect" vernacular of *Huckleberry Finn* is to be more than décor, it must enact an equally "incorrect" vision. Otherwise, the style becomes merely a way of saying rather than a way of being. It is not simply the "poetry" or "beauty" or "rhythm" of Huck's vernacular which makes his language work, but the presence of a commensurate vernacular vision. The reason that imitators of *Huckleberry Finn* fail—the reason that Mark Twain himself later failed—is that they lack the vision to match their style, and thus their language is merely décor. One has but to read Edgar Lee Masters' *Mitch Miller*—which is a "modern" attempt to show what the childhood of Huck and Tom was really like—to know how sentimental such language can be unless it is sustained by a genuinely radical vision. Even Sherwood Anderson's "I Want to Know Why," in many ways the finest example of vernacular vision directly derivative from *Huckleberry Finn,* falls far short of Mark Twain, because its end, though finely climactic, is unfortunately sentimental. The young boy's anguished appeal upon discovering the Jockey with the whore is, after all, just the same old truth we knew all the time.

What then *is* the rebellion of *Huckleberry Finn?* What is it but an attack upon the conscience? The conscience, after all is said and done, is the real tyrant in the book. It is the relentless force which pursues Huckleberry Finn; it is the tyrant from which he seeks freedom. And it is not only the social conscience which threatens Huck, but *any* conscience. The social conscience, represented in the book by the slave-holding society of the Old South, is easily seen and exposed. It is the false conscience. But what of the true conscience which the reader wishes to project upon Huck and which Huck himself is at last on the threshold of accepting? It, too, is finally false. Although the book plays upon the notion that all conscience is finally social, it does not stand on that line; for the action is not defining the conscience so much as rejecting it. Whether the conscience is "lower" social conscience or the "higher" inner conscience, it remains the tyrant which drives its victims into the absurd corners from which they cannot escape. Thus on the one hand, there is the "law" or "right" of slavery from which Jim is trying to escape and against which Huck finds himself in helpless re-bellion. But there are then the "inner" codes which appear as equally absurd distortions. There is Pap's belief in freedom; there is the code of the feud which the Grangerfords and Shepherdsons hold to; there is the "honor" of Colonel Sherburn; and finally there is the "principle" of Tom Sawyer who rises proudly to the defense of Jim because he "is as free as any cretur that walks this earth." In every case the con-science, whether it comes from society or from some apparent inner realm, is an agent of aggression—aggression against the self or against another. Either the means or the excuse by which pain is inflicted, the conscience is both law and duty, erasing the possibility of choice and thereby constraining its victims to a necessary and irrevocable course of action.

From the "Southern" conscience, Huck first attempts to flee. But even in flight from it, borne southward on the great river, his "North-ern" conscience begins to awaken. This is the apparently internal con-science—the Civil War he finds himself engaged in on the raft as it glides deeper and deeper into the territory of slavery, not of freedom. Our moral sentiment approves his flight from his Southern conscience, but with the approval comes the hope that he will discover his North-ern conscience. But it is just here that Huck will not accept the invita-tion. For chapter after chapter he remains the fugitive—in flight from the old conscience and evading the development of a new one.

And the reason he evades it is clear—the conscience is *uncomfort-able.* Indeed, comfort and satisfaction are the value terms in *Huckle-berry Finn.* Freedom for Huck is not realized in terms of political liberty but in terms of pleasure. Thus his famous pronouncement about life on the raft: "Other places do seem so cramped up and smothery, but a raft don't. You feel mighty free and easy and comfortable on a raft." [8] And later, when the King and the Duke threaten to break the peace, Huck determines not to take a stand against them, observing, "What you want, above all things, on a raft, is for everybody to be satisfied, and feel right and kind towards the others." [9] In almost every instance Huck projects the good life in terms of ease, satisfaction, comfort. A satirist would see it in terms of justice; a moralist would have it as a place of righteousness. But a humorist envisions it as a place of good feeling, where no pain or discomfort can enter. This is why Huck does not see clothes, which figure so prominently as the garments of civilization, as veils to hide the body, or as the false dress whereby a fiction of status is maintained. This would be the satiric vision. As far as Huck is concerned, clothes and civilization itself are undesirable because they are essentially *uncomfortable.* "But I reckon I got to light out for the territory," he says as he departs, "because Aunt Sally she's going to adopt me and sivilize me, and I can't stand it." [10] When Huck says he "can't stand it," he is literally referring to the cramped discomfort of submitting to the clothes and quarters of civilization. To be sure, the phrase suggests a vastly wider range of significances, but significances that are inexorably rooted in a logic of feeling, comfort, and bodily satisfaction. The significances are *our* discoveries, which are at once made possible by and anchored to the concrete image of the raft, the boy, and the Negro. The good feeling, comfort, and ease dominating this journey which makes its way through a society of meanness, cowardice, and cruelty are perfectly embodied by the raft adrift upon the river.

This logic of pleasure at the heart of the book must also be at the heart of any "positive" value we may wish to ascribe to the experience of reading it. Most criticism of *Huckleberry Finn,* however, retreats from the pleasure principle toward the relative safety of "moral issues" and the imperatives of the Northern conscience. This flight is made because of the uncomfortable feeling relating to Huck's "evasion," his "escape," and finally his "rejection" of civilization. What Huck is rejecting is, of course, the conscience—which Mark Twain was later to rail at under the name of the "Moral Sense." The conscience, the trap of adult civilization which lies in wait for Huck throughout the novel,

---

[8] *Writings,* XIII, 162. The conscience, on the other hand, is the source of discomfort. As Huck says, ". . . it don't make no difference whether you do right or wrong, a person's conscience ain't got no sense, and just goes for him *anyway.* If I had a yaller dog that didn't know no more than a person's conscience does I would pison him" (*Writings,* XIII, 321).

[9] *Ibid.,* p. 174.

[10] *Ibid.,* p. 405.

is what he is at such pains to evade. It is his successful evasion which we as readers cannot finally face. The reader who rejects the paradox usually does so on the grounds that the book is "just" a humorous book. The one who detects and is disturbed by it is more likely to follow William Van O'Connor's pronouncements about the "dangers" of innocence and the "failure" of moral vision. A weakness in Huck —pontificates O'Connor in his attempt to prove that the book is *not* a great American novel—is that he does not "acknowledge the virtues of civilization and live, as one must, inside it." [11] Huck does acknowledge the virtues, of course, and upbraids himself for being uncomfortable with them.

But far from relying upon such cozy affirmations as O'Connor longs for, the book moves *down* the river into the deeper repressions of slavery, enacting at every moment a conversion of morality into pleasure. Extending the range of humor through the ills, the agonies, and the cruelties of civilization, it shows how much the conscience—whether Northern or Southern—is the negative force leading to acts of violence upon the self or upon another. Huck's "escape" is of course an escape from violence, a rejection of cruelty—his instinct is neither to give nor to receive pain if he can avoid it.

The prime danger to his identity comes at the moment he chooses the developing inner or Northern conscience. This moment, when Huck says "All right, then, I'll *go* to hell," is characteristically the moment we fatally approve, and approve *morally*. But it is with equal fatality the moment at which Huck's identity is most precariously threatened. In the very act of choosing to go to hell he has surrendered to the notion of a *principle* of right and wrong. He has forsaken the world of pleasure to make a moral choice. Precisely here is where Huck is about to negate himself—where, with an act of positive virtue, he actually commits himself to play the role of Tom Sawyer which he *has* to assume in the closing section of the book. To commit oneself to the idea, the *morality* of freeing Jim, is to become Tom Sawyer. Here again is the irony of the book, and the ending, far from evading the consequences of Huck's act of rebellion, realizes those consequences.

Mark Twain's real problem—his real dilemma—was not at all his inability to "face" the issues of slavery; certainly it was not a fear of the society or a failure of moral and political courage which brought Mark Twain to the tight place where Huck had to decide forever and ever. Rather, it was the necessities of his humorous form. For in order to achieve expression of the deep wish which *Huckleberry Finn* em-

[11] William Van O'Connor, "Why *Huckleberry Finn* Is Not the Great American Novel," *College English*, XVII (October, 1955), 8.

bodies—the wish for freedom from any conscience—Mark Twain had to intensify the moral sentiment. The moment there is any real moral doubt about Huck's action, the wish will be threatened. Yet when Huck makes his moral affirmation, he fatally negates the wish for freedom from the conscience; for if his affirmation frees him from the Southern conscience, it binds him to his Northern conscience. No longer an outcast, he can be welcomed into the society to play the role of Tom Sawyer, which is precisely what happens. When he submits to Tom's role, we are the ones who become uncomfortable. The entire burlesque ending is a revenge upon the moral sentiment which, though it shielded the humor, ultimately threatened Huck's identity.

This is the larger reality of the ending—what we may call the necessity of the form. That it was a cost which the form exacted no one would deny. But to call it a failure, a piece of moral cowardice, is to miss the true rebellion of the book, for the disturbance of the ending is nothing less than our and Mark Twain's recognition of the full meaning of *Huckleberry Finn*. If the reader is pushed to the limits of his humor, Mark Twain had reached the limits of his—he had seen through to the end. The disillusion begins not when Tom returns to the stage, but when Huck says "All right, then, I'll *go* to hell"—when our applause and approval reach their zenith. At that moment, which anyone would agree is Mark Twain's highest achievement, Huck has internalized the image of Jim; and that image, whose reality he has enjoyed during the fatal drift downstream, becomes the scourge which shames him out of his evasion. The whole process is disclosed in the lyric utterance leading to his decision. Having written the note to Miss Watson telling where Jim is, Huck feels cleansed and at last able to pray:

> But I didn't do it straight off, but laid the paper down and set there thinking—thinking how good it was all this happened so, and how near I come to being lost and going to hell. And went on thinking. And got to thinking over our trip down the river; and I see Jim before me all the time: in the day and in the night-time, sometimes moonlight, sometimes storms, and we a-floating along, talking and singing and laughing. But somehow I couldn't seem to strike no places to harden me against him, but only the other kind. I'd see him standing my watch on top of his'n, 'stead of calling me, so I could go on sleeping; and see him how glad he was when I come back out of the fog; and when I come to him again in the swamp, up there where the feud was; and such-like times; and would always call me honey, and pet me, and do everything he could think of for me, and how good he always was; and at last I struck the time I saved him by telling the men we had smallpox aboard, and he was so grateful, and said I was the best friend old Jim ever had in the world,

and the *only* one he's got now; and then I happened to look around and
see that paper.

    It was a close place.[12]

This lyrical rehearsal of the journey is also the journey's end. And
the decision which ends it is cast in the positive locution of Tom
Sawyer, not in Huck's essentially negative vernacular.[13] When Huck
says he will go to hell, in five minutes of reading time he is there.
For in this novel, which constantly plays against superstitious here-
afters, there is no fire-and-brimstone hell but only civilization—which
is precisely where Huck finds himself as a consequence of his own
determination.

This dilemma and disillusion are what Mark Twain would not
shrink from, but carried through, though it cost him almost everything
—which is saying it cost him his good humor. In the burlesque chapters, he understandably though precariously turned upon his invention, upon his reader, and upon himself. Yet even here he did not
entirely abandon the pleasure principle, but left his "serious" readers
pleased with themselves instead of the book, their moral complacency
ruffled by nothing more than comfortable indignation at the evasions
of humor.

As for Mark Twain, he had seen through to the end, and it almost
killed him. He never would have so good a humor again. His despair,
having set in at the moment of Huckleberry Finn's affirmation, never
really let up. The only way he could survive was to try to swallow the
joke which became more and more sour the rest of his embattled way.
Having seen the limits of his humor, he turned upon them and railed
at the conscience and the need for self-approval, the twin human characteristics which seemed to make the human race utterly ridiculous
and damned.

And what of Huck? As Nick Carraway said of Gatsby, he came out
all right. He went to the territory because he was true to himself and
to his creator. He didn't go there to lead civilization either, but to
play outside it. Refusing to grow up and tell the lie of the conscience,
he left behind him a novel for all time. It was truly a novel of recon-
struction. First, it had brought into fiction not the Old South but an
entirely new one which the Northern conscience could welcome back
into the Union. And in the process of its humor, it reconstructed the

---

12 *Writings*, XIII, 296-97. Although Huck's language constantly describes his feelings and thoughts, they are so directly wedded to external action and dependent
on it that he seems to have no independent "thought." This passage is the only
extended narrative of such an inner life. Once the decision is made, he hardly reflects upon his past. If he remembers, he keeps it to himself.

13 Huck's most characteristic errors of grammar are, significantly enough, his constant use of the double negative and his persistent confusion of verb tense.

psyche, following the pleasure principle as far as it would go to discover in the southern reaches of the Great River the tyranny of the conscience which keeps the adult in chains and makes his pleasure the enactment of greater and greater cruelty. He had not reached childhood's end, but had disclosed the lie of the adult world. In his last moment he said, "so there ain't nothing more to write about, and I am rotten glad of it, because if I'd 'a' knowed what a trouble it was to make a book I wouldn't 'a' tackled it, and ain't a-going to no more." We of course constantly lecture Mark Twain about having turned away from his true vein of ore. The fact is, however, that he could not turn away but kept trying to do just what we want of him. He kept trying to call Huck back to tell another story. But Huck, though he came docilely, could never tell the truth. He had told all the truth he had to tell in one glorious lie.

Huck Finn and the Metaphors of Society

by Richard Poirier

At the outset the reader might be so beguiled by Huck's narrative voice as to forget not only the metaphoric implications in his language but also that, except for his address to the reader, he is remarkably quiet. He speaks infrequently to anyone else; he is seldom heard in conversation, and he is always inconspicuous in company, even in the "gang." His loneliness, we might say, is a want of conversation, a lack, in terms of the literary problem raised by the book, of dramatic relationships. He listens for sounds from nature and interprets them more confidently than language, which tends to confuse or disturb him. "But I never said so," is one of his characteristic comments. The form of the book itself, an autobiography that is also a kind of interior monologue, testifies to the internalization of his feelings and reactions.

And yet, it is necessary to stress that any Emersonian detachment from society for the companionship of the "stars" would never satisfy Huck (or Mark Twain) for very long. His soliloquies are punctuated with the words "lonesome" and "lonely," ending in the present instance with the direct admission that "I did wish I had some company." Company is announced from below the window in the animal noises of Tom Sawyer, and the first chapter ends with tones of deep companionable satisfaction: "Then I slipped down to the ground and crawled among the trees, and, sure enough, there was Tom Sawyer waiting for me."

The organization of the chapter suggests, with pleasure and excitement, that by joining Tom Huck has escaped social entrapment and achieved a Laurentian kind of "freedom"—"freedom together." But Chapter II, with Tom's incessant talk about rules, gangs, and especially books and authority, only confirms the early hint of an essential solidarity between Tom's world and the Widow's, despite her amused

assurance that Tom will not qualify for her heaven. Tom's world is
dominated by games and fantasies imitated from literature, just as hers
is based on illusions derived from religion and the Bible. His tricks,
the first of which is an exploitation of Jim in Chapter II, are justified
by the "authorities" of boys' games and, by extension, of religion and
social respectability, which sanction Miss Watson's exploitation of Jim
at still another level. Tom's question in Chapter II when they are discussing the conduct of a game—"Do you want to go to doing different
from what's in the books, and get things all muddled up?"—implies
even at this point that an argument with the "authority" of boys'
games is a disruption of accredited social procedures.

The alternatives promised in Chapter II by Tom's gang and its
games to the "civilized" confinements of Chapter I turn out, then, to
be no alternatives at all. Offering confirmation of such a reading,
Chapter III puts into direct juxtaposition the activities of religious,
conservative, respectable society, as embodied in Widow Douglas and
Miss Watson, and the activities of children, based on the authorities
of romantic literature as interpreted by Tom Sawyer. We have before
us the creation in words of a whole society built on games, tricks, and
illusions, and the adult version is only superficially different from the
children's. You play the game without asking literal-minded questions,
play as if it were "for real," or you're a "numb-skull."

The metaphorical equation of the world of adults and of children
indicates the relative eccentricity of Huck. Thus while his treatment
of Jim during the reversal scenes is a matter of playing one of Tom's
tricks, of "playing the game" in the larger sense, his subsequent
apology violates the rules of the game as observed both by children and
adults. Implicit here, in the most placidly comic part of the book, is
what Huck will most painfully discover later: that to give up "trick-
ing" Jim means more than giving up Tom's games. It means, so closely
are they imaginatively connected with adult forms of exploitation,
that he must also believe himself damned to social ostracism and to
Hell.

These significances are not declared nor are they derived merely
from images. They are instead the result very often of the similarity of
phrasing applied first to the Widow and Miss Watson and then to
Tom. The unobtrusiveness by which a parallel is thus established results from the use of phrases having the sound merely of idiomatic
repetitiousness, not uncommon in vernacular literature. For example,
in the first half of Chapter III, in which Huck is advised by Miss
Watson about the advantages of prayer and the Bible, there is a
sequence of phrases applied to religion and its promises ("it warn't
so," "spiritual gifts," "I couldn't see no advantage to it") that in
slightly varied form are applied in the second half to Tom's games

and the romantic books which authorize them ("but only just pretended," "done by enchantment," "I couldn't see no profit in it"). In the first half, Huck's literalness, inseparable from a concern for human profit and loss, makes Miss Watson call him a "fool," just as in the second it leads Tom Sawyer to call him a "numb-skull." The list can be extended by anyone who turns to Chapter III, and the implications are in fact summarized in the final sentence of the chapter by Huck himself: "So then I judged that all that stuff was only just one of Tom Sawyer's lies. I reckoned he believed in the A-rabs and the elephants, but as for me I think different. It had all the marks of a Sunday-school." These concluding remarks make the metaphoric intention of the opening chapters unmistakable. Each side of the comparison is modified by the other. Boys' games as Tom plays them are finally, so the comparisons seem to indicate, as genteel and proper as Miss Watson's religion (he always leaves payment for anything he "steals"), and the social respectability and religion which she represents are, like Tom's games, remote from the requirements of natural, literal, daily experience, from a concern for elementary human feelings that are revealed in Huck's "numb-skull" skepticism both about games and religion.

But it is time to remind ourselves again that as we read we are listening to a voice, not drawing metaphoric diagrams. The voice makes the reading of the metaphors and any effort to determine their weight within the total experience of these chapters extremely difficult. Even at this early point we are uncomfortably aware of a gap between Mark Twain's position, his view, expressed through these metaphors, of society merely as system, and the more socially engaged and eager position of the hero. The gap will ultimately mean that the novel becomes simpler later on than it is here. After the reversal scenes, personal drama is not allowed to intrude into a massive parade of social games and disguises. The sound of Huck's socially involved voice first wavers, then nearly disappears, then returns as a sickly version of what we find in these opening scenes. Here, though, it is heard distinctly enough to make the metaphors amusing and affectionate, however damaging they become if one isolates their implications.

The great difficulty for the reader in the opening chapters is that we feel no confidence in balancing the implications of style, its tendency to repudiate what is at the same time being affectionately rendered. It is no wonder that there are many differences of opinion about the structure of the book and about whether or not it expresses an ultimate surrender to the so-called genteel tradition or a final repudiation of it, and of Hannibal, the so-called Happy Valley of Mark Twain's youth. Those critics who respond weakly, or not at all, to the metaphoric implications of the early chapters ignore as a consequence

the extent to which Mark Twain has begun even here to isolate the
consciousness he values from the society in which it seeks to express
itself. Put simply, it is predictable from the outset that the book must
elect to give its attention either to the development of the hero or to
a review of the environment which forestalls that development. The
two cannot be synchronized. This literary difficulty is what plagued
the author in the summer of 1876, not any discovered contempt of his
own, presumably released only by his trip to the Mississippi in 1882,
for the environments of his youth. His criticisms are already evident
enough in 1876. On the other hand, those who do stress the evidences
of repudiation in the early chapters are apt to miss the complications
brought about by the freedom Mark Twain allows to the more loving,
socially agreeable expressions of his hero. The latter reading is best
represented by Leo Marx, whose criticisms of T. S. Eliot and Lionel
Trilling for approving of the later portions of the novel have been
much admired. But I think the reading he himself offers in his essay
confuses Huck Finn with Mark Twain in the opening chapters, not
letting us see how much Huck's voice modifies the social criticism,
and it then confuses Mark Twain with Huck in the concluding chapters, missing, it seems to me, the degree to which we can only respond
to Huck within what has become by then the author's rigidly bitter
and impersonal metaphoric design.

What happens to this novel is what happens to Huck at the hands
of his creator. The problem for the author after the crucial scenes in
Chapters xv and xvi is that the novel can no longer be the autobiography of Huck Finn. It must instead become a kind of documentation
of why the consciousness of the hero cannot be developed in dramatic
relations to any element of this society. Kenneth Lynn's version of
the problem—that after Chapter xvi Mark Twain discovered he must
damn the Happy Valley and was loath to do so—has already been para-
phrased and questioned in the preceding paragraph. But his reading
of this part of the novel can, with some important modifications, take
us close to the difficulties that the novelist himself must have felt at
this point in the writing. Mark Twain has written himself into a
position where he can no longer sustain a double relationship to the
social environment of his novel—of the remote contemptuous critic, on
the one hand, and, on the other, of the man with illusions that some
closer relationship, such as Huck himself seems to want with Tom,
can be maintained.

Were we to read the last sentences of Chapter iii as Mr. Marx suggests—"With this statement which ends the third chapter, Huck parts
company with Tom"—there would of course be no such problem as I
describe. Without Huck's continued longing for some kind of tie

with Tom ("respectable" society at its most palatable), the novel would be a relatively unmodified criticism of society carried out by Huck himself, until the author, so Mr. Marx's argument runs, in his essay and in *The Machine in the Garden*, forces a surrender to society at the conclusion. Some such development does occur but it is blurred by the fact that Huck is cultivating an imaginative association with Tom (and therefore society) all the way from Chapter III to Chapter XV. He consistently imitates him, and to that extent is, like the rest of this society, imitating "books" and "authorities." He repeatedly cites Tom as his own authority for tricks and adventures that are conspicuously at odds with both his feelings and self-interest. The attractions of social life for Huck, his persistent wish that "I had some company," are never wholly satisfied by the companionship of Jim, which explains why, when they are separated, Huck can so easily put him out of mind. Tom is evoked, however, no matter how lengthy the separation. When he frees himself from Pap, with elaborate trickery in Chapter VII, Huck "did wish Tom Sawyer was there; I knowed he would take an interest in this kind of business, and throw in the fancy touches. Nobody could spread himself like Tom Sawyer in such a thing as that." In Chapter XII, his escapade on the *Walter Scott* is justified to Jim by asking, "Do you reckon Tom Sawyer would ever go by this thing?" and it could be inferred at this point that Jim, as a companion on adventures, is implicitly dismissed by the added remark that "I wish Tom Sawyer *was* here." . . . Huck's imitations of Tom indicate the degree to which he must become an artificial man, an imitator of literary models, if he is to be a part of society at all or be accepted by it as a "real" boy, like Tom.

As the novel moves to the crisis of insult and apology in Chapter XV, "imitation" is shown, just as at Box Hill, to result in the loss of "self-command" and an enslavement to alien forms of expression that distort genuine feelings. Chapter XIV, "Was Solomon Wise?" is a preparatory and comic version of Chapter XV, "Fooling Poor Old Jim." In the first, the imitative tendencies of Huck are developed to a point where, with brilliant comic significance, he has stylistically become Tom Sawyer, while transferring his own identity as a "numb-skull" to Jim ("I said these things was adventures; but he said he didn't want no more adventures"), and he tries to win the argument by citing the Widow ("the Widow told me all about it"). He thus adopts for his "authorities" the two figures who together represent aspects of the artifice which, in this novel, are equivalent to society. Huck, trying to be Tom, bases his arguments on a faith in symbolic actions, regardless of the practical consequences, while Jim, like Huck himself in earlier arguments with the real Tom, insists on them: "En what use is half a chile? I wouldn' give a dern for a million of um." To which Huck replies, much as Tom does to him, "Hang it, Jim, you've clean missed the point."

Huck's imitation and assumption of Tom's role at this point prepares us for the crucial scene about to take place. In the next chapter, after the separation in the fog, Huck continues the tricks begun by Tom in Chapter II. He tries to convince Jim that he has merely been dreaming, that what he believed were naturally stimulated feelings of loss and love were the result rather of fantasy. When Jim realizes that he is being tricked, he responds with a speech that evokes all the affectionate trust that has been evident as the unspoken reality of their relationship. It is only at this point, not at any earlier one, that Huck does separate himself from Tom:

> It was fifteen minutes before I could work myself up to go and humble myself to a nigger—but I done it, and I warn't ever sorry for it afterwards, neither. I didn't do him no more mean tricks, and I wouldn't done that one if I'd 'a' knowed it would make him feel that way.

The nature of Huck's regret here makes his later adoption of Tom's name and his later acceptance of Tom's leadership in the mock freeing of Jim much more than a sacrifice of the emotional growth registered in this passage, much more even than a nearly total collapse of Mark Twain's characterization of the hero. These later developments show the extent to which Mark Twain, no less than his hero, has fallen victim to the world structured by this novel. That the circumstances of Huck's characterization, his environmental placement, make it impossible to sustain the identity he momentarily achieves in the reversal scenes is apparently recognized by Mark Twain himself in the chapter immediately following. The very title of it, "The Rattlesnake-Skin Does its Work," again suggests how Huck's tricks on Jim always do have painfully real consequences. In this chapter we find Huck trapped in verbal conventions that prevent the release of his feelings in words. The terminology he has been taught to use and that binds him to Tom Sawyer and the others cannot let him express the nature of his relationship to Jim. He feels the "pinch of conscience," which is to say the "pinch" of training, of system, of education. ("It [conscience] is merely a *thing*," according to an entry in Mark Twain's notebooks, "the creature of *training;* it is whatever one's mother and Bible and comrades and laws and systems of government and habitat and heredities have made it.") In the novel, conscience is the product of the "games" of comrades and of the "authorities" of books, including the Bible. The meanings which these impart to Huck's language are inadequate to his feelings. Having been defined most significantly for the reader in scenes of flight with a runaway slave, Huck is still enslaved himself to the language of Tom's settled world, still inescapably at-tached to it: "Here was this nigger, which I had as good as helped to run away, coming right out flat-footed and saying he would steal his children—children that belonged to a man I didn't even know; a man that hadn't ever done me no harm."

Huckleberry Finn is an instance of what happens to a novel when society, as the author conceives it, provides no opportunity, no lan-guage, for the transformation of individual consciousness into social drama. The provision is lacking because Mark Twain cannot imagine a society that offers alternatives to artificiality or that has in it, like Joyce's Dublin, evidences of an official culture that has historical dig-nity and value. Huck's problem here represents the crisis in the novel itself. This last quotation, and Huck's use nearby of "right" for what Mark Twain has made us see is "wrong," of "wrong" for "right," in-volves a recognition by the author, more perplexed than any it an-ticipates in Joyce, of what happens when the hero of a novel must define his alienations from society in terms that take their meanings for him, as much as for anyone, from the very "authorities" he has come to reject.

* * *

No wonder Mark Twain could not recognize in the novels of Jane Austen the existence of a society of alternatives. The existence of such a society in her work explains the necessary difference betwen *Emma* and *Huckleberry Finn* revealed at the point in each where the social order is disrupted by an insult. In *Emma,* the crisis results in a restora-tion to social intercourse of a naturalness temporarily lost through artifice; in *Huckleberry Finn* it can lead only to the hero's painful and confused recognition of what his creator has been showing all along—that what is natural for society is in fact nothing but artifice, tricks, games, and disguise. . . . Throughout the rest of the book Huck must move about in various disguises, tell lies, play roles even more than he has before. And he will at last become "Tom Sawyer" all over again in Chapter xxxii. Still more important, the Huck Finn shown to us at what is obviously the dramatic crisis of the book is dis-guised thereafter even from the reader. The style of the book after that carries his voice only sporadically: in some lyrical descriptions of life on the raft, and with significant moral complication only once more—for a moment in Chapter xxxi. The implications are historically important: this novel discovers that the consciousness it values most cannot expand within the environment it provides, that the self can-not come to fuller life through social drama, upon which the vitality of this and of most other novels of the last century at some necessary point depend.

PART TWO

View Points

William Dean Howells

Missouri was Western, but it was also Southern, not only in the institution of slavery, to the custom and acceptance of which Mark Twain was born and bred without any applied doubt of its divinity, but in the peculiar social civilization of the older South from which his native State was settled. It would be reaching too far out to claim that American humor, of the now prevailing Western type, is of Southern origin, but without staying to attempt it I will say that I think the fact could be established; and I think one of the most notably Southern traits of Mark Twain's humor is its power of seeing the fun of Southern seriousness, but this vision did not come to him till after his liberation from neighborhood in the vaster far West. He was the first, if not the only man of his section, to betray a consciousness of the grotesque absurdities in the Southern inversion of the civilized ideals in behalf of slavery, which must have them upside down in order to walk over them safely. No American of Northern birth or breeding could have imagined the spiritual struggle of Huck Finn in deciding to help the negro Jim to his freedom, even though he should be forever despised as a negro thief in his native town, and perhaps eternally lost through the blackness of his sin. No Northerner could have come so close to the heart of a Kentucky feud, and revealed it so perfectly, with the whimsicality playing through its carnage, or could have so brought us into the presence of the sardonic comi-tragedy of the squalid little river town where the store-keeping magnate shoots down his drunken tormentor in the arms of the drunkard's daughter, and then cows with bitter mockery the mob that comes to lynch him. The strict religiosity compatible in the Southwest with savage precepts of conduct is something that could make itself known in its amusing contrast only to the native Southwesterner, and the revolt against it is as constant in Mark Twain as the enmity to New England orthodoxy is in Dr. Holmes. But he does not take it with such serious resentment as Dr. Holmes is apt to take his inherited Puritanism, and it may be therefore that he is able to do it more perfect justice, and impart it more absolutely. At any rate there are no more vital passages in his

From "Mark Twain: An Inquiry" by William Dean Howells. From North American Review, CLXXII (February, 1901), 311-15.

fiction than those which embody character as it is affected for good as well as evil by the severity of the local Sunday-schooling and church-going.

I find myself . . . speaking first of the fiction, which by no means came first in Mark Twain's literary development. It is true that his beginnings were in short sketches, more or less inventive, and studies of life in which he let his imagination play freely; but it was not till he had written *Tom Sawyer* that he could be called a novelist. Even now I think he should rather be called a romancer, though such a book as *Huckleberry Finn* takes itself out of the order of romance and places itself with the great things in picaresque fiction. Still it is more poetic than picaresque, and of a deeper psychology. The probable and credible soul that the author divines in the son of the town drunkard is one which we might each own brother, and the art which portrays this nature at first hand in the person and language of the hero, without pose or affectation, is fine art. In the boy's history the author's fancy works realistically to an end as high as it has reached elsewhere, if not higher; and I who like *The Connecticut Yankee at King Arthur's Court* so much, have half a mind to give my whole heart to *Huckleberry Finn*.

*   *   *

I do not think he succeeds so often with [woman] nature as with the boy nature or the man nature, apparently because it does not interest him so much. He will not trouble himself to make women talk like women at all times; oftentimes they talk too much like him, though the simple, homely sort express themselves after their kind; and Mark Twain does not always write men's dialogue so well as he might. He is apt to burlesque the lighter colloquiality, and it is only in the more serious and most tragical junctures that his people utter themselves with veracious simplicity and dignity. That great, burly fancy of his is always tempting him to the exaggeration which is the condition of so much of his personal humor, but which when it invades the drama spoils the illusion. The illusion renews itself in the great moments, but I wish it could be kept infract in the small, and I blame him that he does not rule his fancy better. His imagination is always dramatic in its conceptions, but not always in its expressions; the talk of his people is often inadequate caricature in the ordinary exigencies, and his art contents itself with makeshift in the minor action. Even in *Huck Finn,* so admirably proportioned and honestly studied, you find a piece of lawless extravagance hurled in, like the episode of the two strolling actors in the flatboat; their broad burlesque is redeemed by their final tragedy—a prodigiously real and moving passage—but the friend of the book cannot help wishing the burlesque was not there.

One laughs, and then despises oneself for laughing, and this is not what Mark Twain often makes you do. There are things in him that shock, and more things that we think shocking, but this may not be so much because of their nature, as because of our want of naturalness; they wound our conventions rather than our convictions. As most women are more the subjects of convention than men, his humor is not for most women; but I have a theory that when women like it they like it far beyond men. Its very excess must satisfy that demand of their insatiate nerves for something that there is enough of; but I offer this conjecture with instant readiness to withdraw it under correction. What I feel rather surer of is that there is something finally feminine in the inconsequence of his ratiocination, and his beautiful confidence that we shall be able to follow him to his conclusion in all those turnings and twistings and leaps and bounds, by which his mind carries itself to any point but that he seems aiming at. Men, in fact, are born of women, and possibly Mark Twain owes his literary method to the colloquial style of some far ancestress who was more concerned in getting there, and amusing herself on the way, than in ordering her steps.

Possibly also it is to this ancestress that he owes the instinct of right and wrong which keeps him clear as to the conditions that formed him, and their injustice. Slavery in a small Missouri river town could not have been the dignified and patriarchal institution which Southerners of the older South are fond of remembering or imagining. In the second generation from Virginia ancestry of this sort, Mark Twain was born to the common necessity of looking out for himself, and while making himself practically of another order of things he felt whatever was fine in the old and could regard whatever was ugly and absurd more tolerantly, more humorously than those who bequeathed him their enmity to it. Fortunately for him, and for us who were to enjoy his humor, he came to his intellectual consciousness in a world so large and free and safe that he could be fair to any wrong while seeing the right so unfailingly; and nothing is finer in him than his gentleness with the error which is simply passive and negative. He gets fun out of it, of course, but he deals almost tenderly with it, and hoards his violence for the superstitions and traditions which are arrogant and active. His pictures of that old rivertown, Southwestern life, with its faded and tattered aristocratic ideals and its squalid democratic realities, are pathetic, while they are so unsparingly true and so inapologetically and unaffectedly faithful.

Van Wyck Brooks

Through the character of Huck, that disreputable, illiterate little boy, as Mrs. Clemens no doubt thought him, he was licensed to let himself go. We have seen how indifferent his sponsors were to the writing and the fate of this book: "nobody," says Mr. Paine, "appears to have been especially concerned about Huck, except, possibly, the publisher." The more indifferent they were, the freer was Mark Twain! Anything that little vagabond said might be safely trusted to pass the censor, just because he was a little vagabond, just because, as an irresponsible boy, he could not, in the eyes of the mighty ones of this world, know anything in any case about life, morals and civilization. That Mark Twain was almost, if not quite, conscious of his opportunity we can see from his introductory note to the book: "Persons attempting to find a motive in this narrative will be prosecuted; persons attempting to find a moral in it will be banished; persons attempting to find a plot in it will be shot." He feels so secure of himself that he can actually challenge the censor to accuse him of having a motive! Huck's illiteracy, Huck's disreputableness and general outrageousness are so many shields behind which Mark Twain can let all the cats out of the bag with impunity. He must, I say, have had a certain sense of his unusual security when he wrote some of the more cynically satirical passages of the book, when he permitted Colonel Sherburn to taunt the mob, when he drew that picture of the audience who had been taken in by the Duke proceeding to sell the rest of their townspeople, when he has the King put up the notice, "Ladies and Children not Admitted," and add: "There, if that line don't fetch them, I don't know Arkansaw!" The withering contempt for humankind expressed in these episodes was of the sort that Mark Twain expressed more and more openly, as time went on, in his own person; but he was not indulging in that costly kind of cynicism in the days when he wrote *Huckleberry Finn*. He must, therefore, have appreciated the license that little vagabond, like the puppet on the lap of a ventriloquist, afforded him. This, however, was only a trivial detail in his general sense of happy expansion, of ecstatic liberation. "Other places do seem so cramped up and smothery, but a raft don't," says Huck, on the river; "you feel mighty free and easy and comfortable

From The Ordeal of Mark Twain *by Van Wyck Brooks (New York: E. P. Dutton & Co., Inc., 1920; London: J. M. Dent & Sons, Ltd., 1920), pp. 194-96. Copyright 1920 by E. P. Dutton & Co., Inc. Renewal copyright © 1948 by Van Wyck Brooks. Reprinted by permission of the publishers.*

on a raft." Mark Twain himself was free at last!—that raft and that river to him were something more than mere material facts. His whole unconscious life, the pent-up river of his own soul, had burst its bonds and rushed forth, a joyous torrent! Do we need any other explanation of the abandon, the beauty, the eternal freshness of *Huckleberry Finn?* Perhaps we can say that a lifetime of moral slavery and repression was not too much to pay for it. Certainly, if it flies like a gay, bright, shining arrow through the tepid atmosphere of American literature, it is because of the straining of the bow, the tautness of the string, that gave it its momentum.

Yes, if we did not know, if we did not feel, that Mark Twain was intended for a vastly greater destiny, for the rôle of a demiurge, in fact, we might have been glad of all those petty restrictions and misprisions he had undergone, restrictions that had prepared the way for this joyous release. No smoking on Sundays! No "swearing" allowed! Neckties having to be bothered over! That everlasting diet of Ps and Qs, petty Ps and pettier Qs, to which Mark Twain had had to submit, the domestic diet of Mrs. Clemens, the literary diet of Mr. Howells, those second parents who had taken the place of his first—we have to thank it, after all, for the vengeful solace we find in the promiscuous and general revolt of Huckleberry Finn.

F. Scott Fitzgerald

Huckleberry Finn took the first journey *back*. He was the first to look *back* at the republic from the perspective of the west. His eyes were the first eyes that ever looked at us objectively that were not eyes from overseas. There were mountains at the frontier but he wanted more than mountains to look at with his restless eyes—he wanted to find out about men and how they lived together. And because he turned back we have him forever.

Written in 1935 on the occasion of the centenary of Mark Twain's birth. Reprinted from Fitzgerald Newsletter *No. 8 (Winter 1960) by permission of its editor, Matthew J. Bruccoli; the text has been collated with the original typescript in the collection of Mr. Bruccoli.*

T. S. Eliot

In *Huckleberry Finn* Mark Twain wrote a much greater book than he could have known he was writing. Perhaps all great works of art

From T. S. Eliot's Introduction to Adventures of Huckleberry Finn *(London: The Cresset Press, 1950). Reprinted by permission of The Barrie Group of Publishers.*

mean much more than the author could have been aware of meaning:
certainly, *Huckleberry Finn* is the one book of Mark Twain's which,
as a whole, has this unconsciousness. So what seems to be the rightness,
of reverting at the end of the book to the mood of *Tom Sawyer,* was
perhaps unconscious art. For Huckleberry Finn, neither a tragic nor
a happy ending would be suitable. No worldly success or social satisfaction, no domestic consummation would be worthy of him; a tragic
end also would reduce him to the level of those whom we pity. Huck
Finn must come from nowhere and be bound for nowhere. His is not
the independence of the typical or symbolic American Pioneer, but
the independence of the vagabond. His existence questions the values
of America as much as the values of Europe; he is as much an affront
to the "pioneer spirit" as he is to "business enterprise"; he is in a
state of nature as detached as the state of the saint. In a busy world,
he represents the loafer; in an acquisitive and competitive world, he
insists on living from hand to mouth. He could not be exhibited in
any amorous encounters or engagements, in any of the juvenile affections which are appropriate to Tom Sawyer. He belongs neither to the
Sunday School nor to the Reformatory. He has no beginning and no
end. Hence, he can only disappear; and his disappearance can only be
accomplished by bringing forward another performer to obscure the
disappearance in a cloud of whimsicalities.

   Like Huckleberry Finn, the River itself has no beginning or end. In
its beginning, it is not yet the River; in its end, it is no longer the
River. What we call its headwaters is only a selection from among
the innumerable sources which flow together to compose it. At what
point in its course does the Mississippi become what the Mississippi
means? It is both one and many; it is the Mississippi of this book only
after its union with the Big Muddy—the Missouri; it derives some of
its character from the Ohio, the Tennessee and other confluents. And
at the end it merely disappears among its deltas: it is no longer there,
but it is still where it was, hundreds of miles to the North. The River
cannot tolerate any design, to a story which is its story, that might
interfere with its dominance. Things must merely happen, here and
there, to the people who live along its shores or who commit themselves to its current. And it is as impossible for Huck as for the River
to have a beginning or end—a *career.* So the book has the right, the
only possible concluding sentence. I do not think that any book ever
written ends more certainly with the right words:

> But I reckon I got to light out for the territory ahead of the rest, because
> Aunt Sally she's going to adopt me and sivilize me, and I can't stand it.
> I been there before.

F. R. Leavis

Huckleberry Finn, by general agreement Mark Twain's greatest work, is supremely the American classic, and it is one of the great books of the world. The significance of such a work doesn't admit of exhaustive recognition in a simple formula, or in several. Mark Twain himself was no simple being, and the complexity of his make-up was ordinarily manifested in strains, disharmonies, and tormenting failures of integration and self-knowledge. These, in his supreme masterpiece, can be seen to provide the creative drive. There is of course the aspect of return to boyhood, but the relation to complexity and strain represented by *Huckleberry Finn* is not one of escape from them—in spite of the qualities that have established the book as a classic for children (and in spite of Mark Twain's conviction, at times, that its appeal should be as such). It is true that the whole is given through Huck, the embodiment of that Western vernacular, or of the style created out of that, in which the book is written. But that style, perfectly as it renders the illiterate Huck, has been created by a highly sophisticated art to serve subtle purposes, and Huck himself is of course not merely the naïve boyish consciousness he so successfully enacts; he is, by one of those triumphant sleights or equivocations which cannot be judiciously contrived, but are proof of inspired creative possession, the voice of deeply reflective maturity—of a life's experience brooded on by an earnest spirit and a fine intelligence. If Mark Twain lacked art in Arnold Bennett's sense (as Arnold Bennett pointed out), that only shows how little art in Arnold Bennett's sense matters, in comparison with art that is the answer of creative genius to the pressure of a profoundly felt and complex experience. If *Huckleberry Finn* has its examples of the unintelligence that may accompany the absence of sustained critical consciousness in an artist, even a great one, nevertheless the essential intelligence that prevails, and from the poetic depths informs the work, compels our recognition—the intelligence of the whole engaged psyche; the intelligence that represents the integrity of this, and brings to bear the wholeness.

For in his supreme creation the complex and troubled Mark Twain did achieve a wholeness; it is manifested in the nature of the creative

From F. R. Leavis's Introduction to Pudd'nhead Wilson *(London: Chatto & Windus, Ltd., 1955). Reprinted in* Anna Karenina and Other Essays, *by F. R. Leavis (London: Chatto & Windus, Ltd., 1967). Reprinted by permission of author and publisher.*

triumph. The charged significance of *Huckleberry Finn* brings together a strength of naïveté and a strength of mature reflective wisdom. Let me quote, with immediate relevance, Mr. Bernard DeVoto,
most penetrating of the commentators on Mark Twain I am ac-
quainted with:

> . . . fundamentally Huck is an expression—a magnificent expression, a
> unique expression—of the folk mind. The folk mind, that is, in mid-
> America in the period of the frontier and immediately following, the folk
> mind shaped for use by the tremendous realities of conquering a hostile
> wilderness and yet shadowed by the unseen world. He is one of the
> highest reaches of American fiction.
>
> But if Huck expresses the folk mind, he is also Mark Twain's surrogate,
> he is charged with transmitting what that dark, sensitive, and complex
> consciousness felt about America and the human race. . . . Mark Twain
> was not a systematic thinker. Customarily, like the creature of fable who
> was his brother Orion, he held in succession all possible opinions about
> every subject he tried to analyze, held none of them long, and was able to
> drive none very deep beneath the surface. Especially as a metaphysician
> he was as feeble a novice as ever ventured into that stormy sea. But in
> what he perceived, in what he felt, in the nerve-ends of emotion, in the
> mysterious ferments of art which transform experience, he was a great
> mind—there has been no greater in American literature. Be it said once
> more and ever so wearily: insufficiencies and defects prevented him from
> ever completely implementing the artist throughout the whole course of
> a book. That does not matter—in *Huckleberry Finn* we get the finest
> expression of a great artist, the fullest report on what life meant to him.[1]

When Mr. DeVoto speaks of the "folk mind" in *Huckleberry Finn*
he is making a plainly valid observation; an observation duly offset, as
the quoted passage shows, by the recognition of quite other aspects of
the book. But insistence on the "folk" element sometimes goes with an
attempt to make *Huckleberry Finn* American in a sense that would
make it an immeasurably lesser thing than the great work it is.
Mr. Van Wyck Brooks writes: "He was the frontier story-teller, the
great folk writer of the American West, and he raised to a pitch un-
rivalled before him the art of oral story-telling and then succeeded in
transferring its effects to paper." [2] Such an account (and there is a formidable representative intention behind it) serves as a license for insist-
ing on the force of the reply—the obvious and unanswerable reply:
Mark Twain was something very much more than a folk-writer, and

---

[1] *Mark Twain at Work* (1942), pp. 99-100.
[2] *The Times of Melville and Whitman* (1947), p. 454. Mr. Brooks says much the
same in *The Ordeal of Mark Twain*.

the art of *Huckleberry Finn* is no mere matter of managing effects—suspense, surprise, climax, and so on. One cannot intelligently discuss the art without discussing the complex and reverse of naïve outlook it conveys. Mr. Brooks, recognizing, as any reader must, an insistent moral preoccupation in the theme, quotes Paine, Mark Twain's biographer: "the author makes Huck's struggle a psychological one between conscience and the law on one side, and sympathy on the other." But there is more to the moral theme of *Huckleberry Finn* than that suggests. What the book conveys is the drama in a mind in which conscience finds that it is not single, and that the "law" doesn't speak with one voice, and that what Paine calls "sympathy" itself engages a moral imperative. In fact, as I have noted elsewhere,[3] *Huckleberry Finn* has as a central theme the complexity of ethical valuation in a society with a complex tradition—a description that applies (for instance) to any "Christian" society.

The book is a profound study of civilized man. And about its attitude towards civilization as represented by the society depicted in it there is nothing simple or simplifying, either in a "frontier" spirit or in a spirit of reductive pessimism. It is not to the point to adduce such private utterances of Mark Twain's as: "We have no real morals, but only artificial ones—morals created and preserved by the forced suppression of natural and healthy instinct." "Never trust the artist; trust the tale": Lawrence's dictum might have been addressed to Mark Twain's case. *Huckleberry Finn,* the tale, gives us a wholeness of attitude that transcends anything ordinarily attainable by the author. The liberation effected by the memories of youth and the Mississippi was, for the creative genius at his greatest, not into irresponsibility but the reverse. The imaginatively recovered vitality of youth ministered, in sum, no more to the spirit of "Pudd'nhead Wilson's Calendar" than to nostalgia or daydream, but to the attainment of a sure and profound moral maturity. That is, to call *Huckleberry Finn* a great work is not an exaggeration.

Richard Chase

The departures from and returns to the river as Huck goes through his adventures approximate the *rite de passage* which in religious cult introduces a boy into manhood, so that in this respect one thinks of

From The American Novel and Its Tradition *by Richard Chase (New York: Doubleday & Company, Inc., 1957), pp. 144-45. Copyright © 1957 by Richard Chase. Reprinted by permission of the publisher.*
[3] In the Introduction to Marius Bewley's *The Complex Fate.*

Huckleberry Finn in relation to the book of Cooper's Mark Twain most disliked—*Deerslayer*, as well as in relation to *The Red Badge of Courage*, Hemingway's *In Our Time*, and Faulkner's *The Bear*. Actually, however, this myth is present in *Huckleberry Finn* only dimly, as a kind of abstract framework or unrealized possibility. This is typical of American literature. Generally speaking, it is not a literature in which the classic actions of the soul as traditionally depicted in myth, religion, and tragedy are carried through. Only in *Deerslayer* and *The Bear* is the drama of initiation rendered with any fullness. Characters in American fiction who seem to be, because of their situation and prospects, candidates for initiation do not usually change much under the pressure of what happens to them and when the author ascribes to his character, as in *The Red Badge of Courage*, a new manhood, new courage, new tragic awareness of life, it sounds unmistakably like "the moral"—in short, an afterthought—and we do not feel that the theme of initiation has been dramatically realized. In looking for the typical American candidates for initiation, one finds either that, sensitive, suffering, and intelligent as they may be, they turn out like Christopher Newman in James's *The American* to be impervious to transformation and tragic awareness or, like Huck Finn himself (or Frederic Henry in *A Farewell to Arms*), they are already initiated, they already know the real world with a tragic awareness. There is no real change in Huck Finn during the course of the book, except that he comes to adopt, as he reflects on his duty to Jim, a morality based on New Testament ethic rather than the convention of his time and place. This is a great achievement but it doesn't make a myth of initiation. What we have is only some of the abstract framework of this myth and some of its poetic awareness of the presence of deity in nature.

Ralph Ellison

I use folklore in my work not because I am Negro, but because writers like Eliot and Joyce made me conscious of the literary value of my folk inheritance. My cultural background, like that of most Americans, is dual (my middle name, sadly enough, is Waldo).

I knew the trickster Ulysses just as early as I knew the wily rabbit of Negro American lore, and I could easily imagine myself a pint-sized Ulysses but hardly a rabbit, no matter how human and resourceful or

Negro. And a little later I could imagine myself as Huck Finn (I so nicknamed my brother) but not, though I racially identified with him, as Nigger Jim, who struck me as a white man's inadequate portrait of a slave.

My point is that the Negro American writer is also an heir of the human experience which is literature, and this might well be more important to him than his living folk tradition. For me, at least, in the discontinuous, swiftly changing and diverse American culture, the stability of the Negro American folk tradition became precious as a result of an act of literary discovery. Taken as a whole, its spirituals along with its blues, jazz and folk tales, it has . . . much to tell us of the faith, humor and adaptability to reality necessary to live in a world which has taken on much of the insecurity and blues-like absurdity known to those who brought it into being.

Philip Young

Each mark leaves a scar: these are not passing upsets for Huck. About the picture of the slaves who are being separated he says, "I can't get it out of my memory." And the sight of Buck Grangerford and his cousin being shot to death as they swam along in the water, already hurt:

> made me so sick I most fell out of the tree. I ain't a-going to tell *all* that happened—it would make me sick again to do that. I wished I hadn't ever come ashore that night to see such things. I ain't ever going to get shut of them—lots of times I dream about them.

The aspect of these brutal episodes that is most relevant to the main plot of a boy going down a river on a raft is quite simply this: that they serve to *wound* him. His experience of violence is tied together, and given its total meaning, by this result alone: violence has made him sick. Innumerable readers have tried it, but the plain truth is that Huckleberry Finn, boy or book, cannot really be understood without this clear perception. *Now* we may look at what has happened to this uncomplicated "child of nature." He may be still "unspoiled," but from having been knocked about so much he is very bruised. Better he had never come ashore that night to see such things, but he came. Now exposed to more bloodshed, drowning and sudden death than he can handle, he is himself their casualty. And Twain—working from

From Ernest Hemingway: A Reconsideration *by Philip Young (University Park, Pa.: Pennsylvania State University Press, 1966), pp. 228-29. Copyright © 1966 by Philip Young. Reprinted by permission of author and publisher.*

his own bitter experience—could predict with unhappy confidence: he isn't ever going to get shut of them. Lots of times he dreams about them.

There are other things besides bad dreams which interfere with Huck's peace. Among them are a very active mind which he cannot put to rest, and a growing bitterness about human nature. He cannot sleep, he tells us: "I couldn't, somehow, for thinking." His encounter with the frauds called the Duke and the Dauphin is supposed to be funny. But Huck is not amused; they disgust him with mankind in general. He is wounded, and bitter, and suffering from both insomnia and nightmare, and he rebels. His rebellion brings the crisis of the novel when he, utterly perplexed and sickened by his experiences, tries to decide whether he will "steal a poor old woman's nigger" or protect him. He is all conflict, and tries to pray, but the words won't come. Finally, tortured, he decides. He will protect the slave, although to him this means taking up wickedness again, and eternal punishment in the hereafter. He has deserted the values of the society of his time.

This is of course his second desertion, really. Completely dissatisfied with his pious foster mother and the effeminate respectability which surrounded her, he had already run away from St. Petersburg. Now, off on his own, and exposed to the violence and evil of society as a whole, he renounces it. He goes on now outside its ways. If it is good, he is wicked. And if it aims for heaven, he will go elsewhere.

Chronology of Important Dates

Samuel L. Clemens	Cultural and Historical Events
1835 Samuel L. Clemens born in Florida, Mo.; 1839, family removed to Hannibal, Mo.	
1848-57 Printer on newspapers in Hannibal, towns in Iowa, New York City, Philadelphia, and Cincinnati.	
1850	Fugitive slave law passed by Congress.
1850-60	Railroads reached the Mississippi River during this decade.
1857-61 Mississippi River steamboat pilot; apprenticeship under Horace Bixby.	
1861-64 Nevada years as miner and Virginia City *Territorial Enterprise* reporter.	Civil War begins (1861). Nevada admitted to Union (1864).
1864-67 Newspaper work in San Francisco; correspondent for Sacramento *Union* and San Francisco *Alta California.*	
1865	Civil War ends.
1867 *Quaker City* Cruise to Europe and the Holy Land.	
1869 *The Innocents Abroad* published.	
1870 Married Olivia Langdon (d. 1904); after brief editorship of Buffalo *Express* settled in Hartford, 1871.	Bret Harte's western stories brought him national acclaim.
1871-81	*Atlantic Monthly* edited by W. D. Howells.

1872	*Roughing It* published.
1873	*The Gilded Age,* with C. D. Warner.
1875	"Old Times on the Mississippi" articles for the *Atlantic Monthly*.
1876	*Tom Sawyer* published; *Huckleberry Finn* begun.
1878-79	European residence and travel; *A Tramp Abroad* published, 1880.
1882	Trip down Mississippi River.
1883	*Life on the Mississippi* published; *Huckleberry Finn* completed.
1884	Established his own publishing house, Charles L. Webster & Co.; *Huckleberry Finn* published in England (American ed., 1885).

1885   Howells' *Rise of Silas Lapham* and Henry James's *The Bostonians* published.

1889   *A Connecticut Yankee in King Arthur's Court* published.

1891-95   European residence; deepening involvement with publishing house and Paige typesetter.   International Copyright Act (1891).

1893   Financial panic.

1894   Financial failure; recouped largely by round-the-world lecture tour, 1895-96, and *Following the Equator*, 1897; renewed residence in Europe, 1897-1900.

1898   Spanish-American War; problems of American imperialism debated.

1900   Residence in New York City; built Stormfield, near Redding, Connecticut, 1908.

1906   Began autobiographical dictations.

1910   Died, April 21, at Stormfield; buried in family plot, Elmira, New York.

Notes on the Editor and Contributors

CLAUDE M. SIMPSON, the editor, is Coe Professor of American Literature at Stanford University. He is a general editor of the Centenary Edition of the Works of Nathaniel Hawthorne.

RICHARD P. ADAMS is Professor of English at Tulane University.

GLADYS CARMEN BELLAMY is Professor of English, Emeritus, at Southwestern State College, Weatherford, Oklahoma, and the author of *Mark Twain as a Literary Artist* (1950).

WALTER BLAIR, Professor of English at the University of Chicago, is the author of *Mark Twain & Huck Finn* (1960), *Horse Sense in American Humor* (1942), and the editor of *Native American Humor* (1937).

VAN WYCK BROOKS (1886-1963) was a prolific critic and literary historian. Among his books are *The Ordeal of Mark Twain* (1920; rev. ed., 1933), *America's Coming of Age* (1915), and the five volumes of the *Makers and Finders* series (1936-52).

RICHARD CHASE (1914-1962) was the author of *The American Novel and Its Tradition* (1957), *Walt Whitman Reconsidered* (1955), *Herman Melville* (1949), and other works.

JAMES M. COX is Professor of English at Dartmouth College and the author of *Mark Twain: The Fate of Humor* (1966).

BERNARD DEVOTO (1897-1955) was Albert Bigelow Paine's successor as custodian of the Mark Twain papers, and from his researches came *Mark Twain at Work* (1942), as well as his editions of *Mark Twain in Eruption* (1940) and *Letters from the Earth* (prepared in 1939, published 1962).

T. S. ELIOT (1888-1965), the celebrated poet, critic, editor, and playwright, wrote the introduction for an edition of *Huckleberry Finn* (1950).

RALPH ELLISON is the author of *Invisible Man* (1952) and a collection of essays, *Shadow and Act* (1964).

F. SCOTT FITZGERALD (1896-1940) is chiefly remembered for his novels, *The Great Gatsby* (1925) and *Tender Is the Night* (1934).

WILLIAM DEAN HOWELLS (1837-1920) was Mark Twain's lifelong friend and literary adviser. He reviewed most of Twain's books—but not *Huckleberry*

117

Finn—and included a selection of his criticisms along with a warm personal memoir in *My Mark Twain* (1910).

F. R. LEAVIS, Director of English Studies and Fellow of Downing College, Cambridge University, has written many books including *The Great Tradition* (1948), and was a moving force behind the influential journal *Scrutiny* (1932-53).

LEO MARX, author of *The Machine in the Garden* (1964), is Professor of English and of American Studies at Amherst College.

RICHARD POIRIER, Professor of English at Rutgers University, is an editor of *Partisan Review* and the author of *A World Elsewhere* and *The Comic Sense of Henry James* (1960).

GILBERT M. RUBENSTEIN is Professor of English at Pace College in New York City.

HENRY NASH SMITH is Professor of English at the University of California, Berkeley. He is the author of *Mark Twain: The Development of a Writer* (1962), *Virgin Land* (1950), and editor (with William M. Gibson) of *Mark Twain-Howells Letters* (1960).

PHILIP YOUNG, author of *Ernest Hemingway: A Reconsideration* (1966; original edition 1952), is Professor of English at Pennsylvania State University.

Selected Bibliography

Walter Blair's *Mark Twain & Huck Finn* (1960), the fullest study of the novel, contains also an extensive bibliography of *Huckleberry Finn* criticism and comment. General bibliographies are also included in *Eight American Authors: A Review of Research and Criticism,* ed. Floyd Stovall, with a supplement by J. Chesley Mathews (1960). Albert Bigelow Paine's *Mark Twain: A Biography* (1912) has the strengths and weaknesses of an authorized work. To it should be added Dixon Wecter's *Sam Clemens of Hannibal* (1952) for the important formative years. DeLancey Ferguson's *Mark Twain: Man and Legend* (1943) is sound and compact. Justin Kaplan's *Mr. Clemens and Mark Twain* (1966), though occasionally marred by factual errors and psychoanalytical speculation, is highly readable. Van Wyck Brooks's challenging view of the frontier and the artist in *The Ordeal of Mark Twain* (1920) was slightly revised (1933) after Bernard DeVoto's rebuttal of Brooks in *Mark Twain's America* (1932); the controversy has been well summarized, with documentary extracts, in *A Casebook on Mark Twain's Wound,* ed. Lewis Leary (1962). Other studies of interest include Louis J. Budd, *Mark Twain: Social Philosopher* (1962); Kenneth Lynn, *Mark Twain and Southwestern Humor* (1959); Franklin R. Rogers, *Mark Twain's Burlesque Patterns* (1960); and Albert E. Stone, Jr., *The Innocent Eye: Childhood in Mark Twain's Imagination* (1961).